Unraveled

Unraveled

Ellie Martinez

ELLIE MARTINEZ

Cover photo by James Baldwin on Unsplash

For my sister, Jessica. You inspire me.

Table of Contents

1 - Rebecca

I often imagine myself driving across the warm open plains of Texas or winding my way along the coast of California, the sea roaring in my ears. Megan talks about places like that all the time and I plead with her over the distance of a telephone call for more details so I can take myself there and just disappear. Maybe I could see Mount Rushmore, feel the dry sandy earth under my feet and the heat on my skin as I stare up at a masterpiece. One of my favorite imaginary places is not even an actual place. It's a fictional moment in time. I'm holding hands with the man that I love, walking somewhere and it doesn't matter where because we're together. Our child is trotting along in front of us asking endless questions and I am so unbelievably happy that is overwhelms my senses. What a fool I am.

This is one of those moments where I wish I could vanish into thin air and reappear at one of those beautiful places or to the life I dream about. But instead, I'm here, at Radio Shack. We've needed batteries for three weeks and now we're finally here and he's looking at stereo equipment.

I sigh at my dismal reality. "Nicholas, we really need batteries." If he's going to get a stereo then I should be able to get a new cell phone.

"Check this out." This is where he pretends that he didn't hear me. "It's got four speakers that you can attach to any wall in the house and a remote." Perfect, another remote so you don't have to get off your ass to turn up the music. Just what we need.

"Cool. Nicholas, c'mon we should get going. Hey! I love these things; we could really use this." It's one of those mini vacuums that picks up everything and you don't have to drag out the big vacuum to clean up. It's just one of those things that I have always wanted to have in the house but just never got around to buying. There was always something better to spend the thirty bucks on, usually things that he wanted.

"We don't need that; we have a vacuum. What are we here for again?" His voice edgy.

"Batteries."

"Batteries? What for, we have tons of batteries."

"They are all dead Nicholas. Remember when the power went out during the storm last week and I was home by myself. No flashlight, I'm stuck in the dark . . . ring a bell?"

"Oh yeah, I got bitched out for an hour about that."

"A half hour – and it was scary okay."

"Whatever. Get the fucking batteries."

"Excuse me? If you're going to be an ass about it then we can just leave."

For a split second the look in his eyes was both superiority and anger swirling together like a tornado. His eyes sometimes seem as smooth and comforting as the sound of the sea and other times like turbulence tossing me around like a rag doll. We were in the corner between the stereo equipment and the batteries, which were hanging in neat little columns on a separate stand. How fitting. As I turned to storm out of the store, he grabbed me hard by the shoulders and shook me, pushing me against the shelves of stereo equipment. I avoided his eyes while another version of myself rose from my body peering down at this couple that was no longer us, no longer who I wanted to be.

"What the fuck is your problem Bec? You don't talk to me like that – ever." He spoke in an angry whisper, which is almost worse than yelling, his eyes darting side to side in between words to be sure no one was watching. I can't believe this is over batteries, what am I doing?

"What? Like what?" I said, trying to diffuse the situation.

"You know what? I was just trying to have a nice relaxing day off with you and you're the one that wanted to come here in the first place. I could be out with Jason golfing right now."

Where did I go wrong? Where did the day get lost in this mess and how did it start over batteries? I should have just let him go golfing instead of talking him into shopping. I should have known better. The only way out was to pretend like his actions didn't affect me. We both have our own defense mechanisms that help us cope; this had become mine.

"Fine, just calm down okay. Let's go." I grabbed the batteries and walked up to the counter, trying to avoid eye contact with the cashier. His name was Kyle or at least that's what his nametag said. I just focused on that. He had to have noticed our little argument in the corner and all of the sudden I felt embarrassed. I leaned on the counter and turned to Nicholas because he carries the money, not me.

"Nicholas." He turns around and looks at me as if to say 'what do you want now'.

"Yes dear?"

"I need some cash."

"Oh yeah, hold on." He digs into his jeans which I start to notice are stained with paint and dirt and only God knows what else. "Here ya go."

He smiles at me and puts down a crumpled up ten-dollar bill on the counter then looks at Kyle and nods; that nod that only guys can do.

"Thanks." I give the ten-dollar bill and batteries to Kyle and a couple of minutes later we are walking out of the store, batteries in hand.

He puts his arm around me and says, "You wanna get something to eat?"

"Sure, I'm starving." I guess everything is okay now.

I've known him since we were kids, eleven or twelve walking the dirt roads of a small town in western Montana without a care in the world. He rode up on a white horse one summer and gave me a rose, how perfect can you get? I thought about the fairytale and grabbed it, clinging to the fibers of my memory with all my might. Since that moment, there has always been a bond between us. So here we are in Denver. We've been dating for about three years, if you don't count the summers spent together years before our official date. Nicholas always made me feel like I was the only one in the world that mattered. I thought back to those times when the

3

only things that seemed to matter in life were a warm sunny day at the river and moonlit walks on a dirt road.

~

"I'll get it!" I ran to the door anticipating who I desperately wanted it to be.

"Nicholas! Hey, I'll get my stuff." It is summer time in Montana, my favorite time of year, especially since there is no school. "Mom! I'm going to the river with Nicholas. I'll be back for dinner."

"Whoa! Rebecca, where on the river are you going?" Mom always wanted all the details. I hated it at the time but looking back she was good at that stuff, responsibility, organization, keeping me entertained when I was little.

"Down by Chief Looking Glass, by the park. We'll stay in that area."

"Okay, be careful and watch for cars on the way down."

"Got it. Bye."

I grabbed my inner tube, towel and hat and ran out the door. I wore my favorite river shoes; old canvas shoes that smelled like summer and looked like they had survived a million trips down the river. Nicholas and I talked all the way down to the river about school, friends, what we wanted to do, where we wanted to live, hobbies, and what we wanted out of life. Grown-up dreams I was anxious to live out. We spoke of everything and nothing all at once. It was a dry, hot day – perfect for tubing. We floated down the river for hours and as we were walking back home, our water-soaked shoes squeaking, he kissed me. It was something I didn't expect but my stomach was in knots and my heart pounding. I must have blushed because he smiled and turned to keep walking, leaving me speechless in the dust and the heat, wanting more. I tried to collect my thoughts and skipped to catch up to him looking straight ahead as if it didn't faze me.

"So, what does your family have planned for the summer?" I didn't want to talk about what just happened because I didn't want him to think it was a big deal since he'd had a girlfriend before.

"Nothing really. My family has their own things going on. I can pretty much do whatever I want. I thought we could pretty much spend the summer together, if you want." He trailed off at the end, a little shy, which I liked. So that's what we did, a summer filled with tubing, talking, walking and just having fun and getting to know each other. I knew even back then that I would marry him one day.

Toward the end of the summer, I was standing in his yard talking to a friend who lived down the street and out of the corner of my eye I saw a white horse. This caught my attention because I've always loved horses, I feel most like myself when I am with them. Living in Montana my family has always had horses and I have been riding since I can remember. Someday I will have a farm of my own here with a family of my own. On top of the white horse was Nicholas, with a red rose. He leaned down and handed me the most beautiful flower I had ever seen. I didn't know what to say, I was speechless living every girl's dream at my age. All I know is everything else around me disappeared and at that moment I felt completely loved for the first time in my life.

2 - Nicholas

What was the big deal about marriage anyway? Becca has been bugging me about asking her since we graduated from high school and it's been getting increasingly obvious over the past year we've been living together. We moved to Denver right out of high school since I was accepted into the University of Colorado. I always wanted get the hell out of Montana and this was my chance. I was perfectly happy with the way things were, but she gave me the impression that we were wasting our time together unless it was *going somewhere*. Why couldn't we just stay where we were? Why did we have to *go somewhere*? It's been a year today since we moved here and only three agonizing years of school to go. We just finished a day of shopping, which I completely detest but had endured for her benefit and she still wasn't happy.

"Becca, what's the problem? We went shopping, we had lunch, was there something else you wanted to do?"

"No."

"Well, then what's with the sullen face?"

"Nothing I just...don't you think you were even remotely rude earlier in Radio Shack?"

"Are you kidding? You're bringing that up? Becca you're the one that pushed *me*. Just stop okay. I'm trying to enjoy the rest of my day off."

"Fine."

There were times when she could push me so far that I wanted to scream and other times just the way she moved around a room drove me crazy and I'd be reminded of how much I love her. I could never stay mad at her for long and she rarely stayed mad at me for more than a couple of hours. I liked that I had that effect on her. It was rare that we had a day off together. I'm in school and she works two jobs most days to help make ends meet. My parents were never much help in the financial department since they could barely feed themselves, so I was doing it all on my own.

I hated that Becca works as a waitress. I preferred her job as a checker in a grocery store but she only works there one or two days a week. I can just picture all the guys drooling over her as they order their food and drinks. I keep telling her that someday she won't have to work at all. *My wife will be home with the kids.* She was giddy at just the mention that we would have kids one day and the fact that I said *wife*. I think it reassured her that she would be in my life. What she didn't understand was that, married or not she would always be a part of my life. It was as if she thought the bottom of our world would fall out from under her at any moment. I love her and we are connected in a way that no one else could ever understand. What fool would want to let that go?

3 - Rebecca

Nicholas was never the suave and charming, tall dark and handsome type but I think that's what attracted me to him. We became very distant during freshman year, maybe it was because we now had to appear cool and different, I'm not sure what it was. We sort of drifted apart without ever fighting and settled into our own group of friends. I still thought about those summers every time I caught a glimpse of him in the busy hallways.

It was junior year in high school shop class of all places, where we discovered the new versions of ourselves and how we could come together again as I secretly always knew we would. I have always been a little more of a tomboy and thought it would be fun to build something. At least I would stay awake in *this* class. My dad is good at building things and it has always fascinated me how an object or building can start out looking shapeless and dull and turn into a beautiful masterpiece with purpose and movement. At one time I wanted to be an architect. Nicholas had a shyness about him that intrigued me because I was usually the one waiting for the other person to say something, and with him, there was a connection, something that pulled me toward him in a way I had never experienced. He brought out a part of me that I never knew existed or could exist until that day in shop class. I had power, strength and confidence that I was not aware of and I liked the way it felt. I liked that he gave that to me.

"You know, you're gonna need an extra clamp for that."

I was trying to maneuver the clamps around my project so that it would lay flat. My long dark hair was in my face as I leaned forward. All I could see were his feet. Work boots or hiking boots with various stains that told a story, gave away their history in a glance. I gave up on the clamps and looked up.

"What?"

"I said you'll need an extra clamp. It won't lay flat when it dries unless you put another clamp in the middle – here I'll show you."

"Oh, yeah." I brushed the hair back from my face and glanced up at him attempting my version of flirting, an awkward concept for me. I knew I should have curled it or done something girly with it today but instead it was straight and boring. He grabbed a clamp from the bucket of tools under the table and started putting it in its proper place. I couldn't help but notice how easy it came to him; where things should go, how to put it together. I always have to put a lot of thought into things to get them right.

"You're pretty handy."

"Yeah? Thanks, I do a lot around the house, fixing things up and that sort of thing."

I wanted to probe a little into personal conversation to see if he was interested but nothing came out. It was dead quiet for a while then he did what I was hoping he would do just as the bell rang.

"So, uh…maybe, if you want you could have lunch with me? Sit with me and have lunch? I guess it's been a while since we've hung out." I could tell he was nervous and although I felt sorry for him, I liked that I made him a little nervous and took it as a good sign. I accepted as casually as I could.

The first thing I did after school was tell Megan every detail of my encounter with Nicholas. She was excited for me, reveling in bliss right alongside me but remained cautious as she often was about many things.

She has been my best friend since I was old enough to walk, I think. We spent countless nights at each other's houses and countless days exploring the Montana countryside and letting our imaginations run wild. Even now, in high school, we have remained close. Sometimes I think we become even closer as we grow up, knowing each other's fears and history seems to give us a connection that is irreplaceable. Megan has always been everything I'm not but that has never stood in the way of our friendship. Somehow, we manage to find a balance without working at it.

Megan is a natural student and not happy unless she is challenged. She is more slender and taller than I am by at least three inches and much more graceful than I could ever hope to be.

Her striking green eyes get the attention of every guy we pass but she never seems to notice because that's Megan, humble and strong. She's always had direction in her life, something I only allowed myself to envy when I was feeling extra pitiful. I knew that whatever she decided to do with her life after high school she would do it well and love every minute of it. We hung out every day after school either studying or just goofing off (when I could convince her to leave the books) and often laughed so hard my cheeks would be sore from smiling for so long. She was the sister I never had and my role model for a social life. We would do anything for each other and she was always there for me even when she didn't agree with me.

My first actual date with Nicholas was not until about six months later when I turned 16. My parents had always told me I had to wait until I was a senior but I convinced them to let me go out with Nicholas after my sixteenth birthday because his parents went to our church and Mom and Dad were familiar with him and his family. I don't think I could have waited a minute longer. My friends were already going out and had all sorts of stories and I longed to have moonlit walks by the river, to catch a movie and make out in the back row, go out to eat and all the other things that couples did. I was bursting at the seams with anticipation.

Walking the dirt roads, it took exactly 16 minutes to walk to his house. I timed it to the second. He showed up at my house on a beautiful cool evening in May. I could just start to smell summer coming. Some people don't think you can smell seasons but I can. I have always been able to smell the rain before it comes, and in the winter, the snow. When a storm passes through, I can smell the sweet damp heat from the lighting. That day I had butterflies in my stomach all through school and throughout dinner. I had to call Megan twice that evening just to get help collecting myself. I'm not sure why. Nicholas and I practically grew up together and had spent time together at school, as well as after school just hanging out, but tonight was different, special somehow, I guess. I was both anxious and nervous at what the future held for me – for us.

4 - Megan

"Becca, you shouldn't put up with that. Give me a break; he doesn't need to call you every second but a little respect is not too much to ask. A call to say he might be home at two in the morning might be helpful." What the hell is she doing? Is she seeing this happen in front of her eyes or does she just think it will all go away?

She has been married to this guy for around three years now and I have no idea how she's stuck it out this long, she should have kicked him to the curb years ago. I knew from her first date that the potential for this relationship to be a chaotic, obsessive, controlling mess was high. I guess I was just hoping that she would grow out of that obsession, that need for him but she never did. She is drawn to him despite the fact that he often fails to reciprocate in any way. She deserves to be adored and supported and he can't and evidently doesn't *want* to give that to her.

"He was out at the bar with Dan playing pool. He got there at four in the afternoon! He just yelled at me and told me that I'm the wife and I should be the one that cooks the meals and shouldn't ask questions because he is the man of the household. I guess he can do whatever the hell he wants to do and I'm just stuck here like a lamp waiting to be turned on."

My husband is talking to me. "Babe, who is that?"

"It's Becca," I whisper, "I'll hurry." We were on our way out the door to go visit my grandparents. Living here in Arizona for the past couple of years we have become so close to them, they are our best friends along with that piece of family that ties it all together. I gave him that look like 'trust me – I got it' and he nods. Sometimes I swear we could communicate without even talking.

"Becca, I'm telling you, you have to kind of play hard to get a little. You can't be the one waiting for him all the time. Ignore him a little and try not to let him know that it bothers you so much. I think he likes the chaotic attention and he takes you for granted." I try to get all my comments in while I can especially if I can't talk long.

"Well, it just frustrates me and I know that he needs to go out with the guys and have fun too –."

"Yeah, Becca, can I call you back later tonight? I'm so sorry but we were on our way out."

"Oh yeah, that's fine. I have to finish doing laundry and vacuuming anyway. I'll talk to you later tonight or tomorrow."

"Okay, cool. Bye."

"Bye." I let out a sigh. Not a sigh of relief but of release. It upsets me beyond belief to hear all the crap that Nick pulls. It's ridiculous, there are neon signs all over the place that should be telling her to stop now, turn around while you still can! Obviously, I know there is nothing I can do for her but be there and try to put in my two cents but I just can't help but be annoyed. I am a strong believer that all the signs for a good or bad relationship are right in front of you from the beginning. It's just a matter of whether you are willing to open your eyes and see them or not. Take Nick and Becca for instance, since they were kids it wasn't meant to be. I could tell because it was obvious that he didn't love her the way she loved him. She has always put much more into it than he did. He's always only done what he had to do to keep her around.

"You ready?" My husband asks waiting at the door with my purse in hand.

"Yeah." I love him. After four years he still takes my breath away.

5 - Nicholas

Since I was a junior shop class, I knew I wanted to be an architect. There are very few things in life that I have found to 'just make sense'. Being an architect was one of them and Becca was the other. Amazingly enough both of these things began my junior year in high school. I remembered Becca from when we were kids going to the river but I never really thought of us as an *us*. It was more fun than anything. I wanted to be liked and she was pretty and funny and seemed to always want to be around me and that was enough at the time. School came and time went on and then one day in shop class I saw her and was shocked that she would be in this class of all places. I stopped what I was doing and watched her struggle with the clamp a little. Her dark brown hair was long to the middle of her back and fell in her face as she bent over the project. She had larger breasts than I thought she would and I wondered why I never noticed her before. She wasn't stick thin and prissy like most of the other girls in our class. She was shorter than me and had a waist that dipped in and beautiful almost hourglass hips. You could tell she was one of those girls that would get prettier as she got older. I just had to walk over and talk to her.

Now here I am six years later with Becca as my wife and a job as an architect in a small firm in Denver. I'm very good at what I do and I worked my ass off every step of the way to get what I wanted. Becca worked as a waitress at two restaurants and as a checker at Whole Foods during my four years of college. I would have liked to wait until I graduated before getting married but she insisted on it being earlier. A year after we graduated from high school, we tied the knot and I had never been so nervous in all my life. Looking back on it now, it was more of a party than a wedding but what did she expect from a kid right out of high school?

Denver is full of organic and health-nut places like Whole Foods, which I was really never too fond of. I'm more of a steak and potatoes, home-cookin' kind of a guy. Growing up in Montana that's what we had and I can't help but have a soft spot for real home-made meals. Over the years we have been here I keep encouraging her to cook more, she is so good at it.

She has the idea that she worked harder than I did during my college years but she's never been to school so she has no clue what it takes to succeed in this world. I appreciate her contribution but *I'm* the one who got me where I am.

6 - Rebecca

I imagined it was raining outside as I stepped out of the grocery store and made my way to the car. The weather in Denver is sporadic and sometimes very unpredictable so I was hoping for a miracle. I would have given anything to hear the rain hit my windshield and watch it form in puddles on the asphalt. Instead of smelling sweet dampness in the air and feeling the weight of gray clouds, all I could see was pure blue sky and all I could smell was hot asphalt from the store parking lot. I needed the weather to match my mood and only one word came to mind; melancholy. But no, instead it is the 'perfect' day. Sunny and warm, the kind of day where parents take their kids to the lake and the high school kids sneak alcohol in their coolers and pile into someone's truck and of course, head to the water.

It is what Nicholas and I would have been doing had reality not steam-rolled into our lives. This morning was going so well and then it was gone in a moment of pure stupidity. Since it's the weekend we both slept in a little. It was one of those mornings where I woke up wonderfully comfortable and Nicholas put his arm around me still half asleep. I was awake but I just laid there savoring every moment. Sometimes in the throes of the stuff of life I feel like we don't get to be close to each other very often. In his arms when the day had not begun, I felt as if I could start over and everything would be okay. I felt like he needed me next to him. When we woke up, we stayed in bed for a few minutes laughing. We had gotten home late the night before from a friend's house and evidently left the lights on all night long. These are the moments I cling to.

You must have been really tired.

I should have read between the lines when he said that, but in our laughter and ease of the morning, I must have tossed it aside refusing to believe that the Nicholas I feared would return. Megan says all the signs are there if you are willing to see them, but I don't get it. It's trickier than that, complicated and gray. She makes it sound so black and white. It was the *you* I should have picked up on. Nothing is ever his fault. Later that afternoon, I finished cleaning up after lunch and Nicholas was freshening up after mowing the front lawn. I planned to ask him if he wanted to go down to the river, maybe take a dip in the cool water or take some snacks down. He had said he wanted to go golfing with Jason earlier but it had been such a nice morning together I thought he might change his mind and spend the rest of the day with me. I approached the subject gingerly as I had learned to do over the past couple of years.

I called up the stairs. "Nicholas?"

"What?" He called back as if he didn't hear me, which I doubted. We are renting a small two-story house and he probably could have heard me from outside the walls are so thin. I let it go and started walking up the stairs with dirty laundry in my arms ready to go in the washer.

"What do you think about maybe going to the river today?"

"Bec, I made plans with Jason to go golfing." He grabbed one of his new polos from the closet and put it over his head. I walked to the small closet where the washer and dryer were and emptied my arms.

"You made plans? I thought you had just mentioned that you were interested. Well anyway, I thought you might change your mind about going. It's the perfect day and I'm sure he would understand right?" He came around the corner dressed to golf in preppy slacks and a Nike golf polo with his new golf shoes in hand.

"Wrong. Hello! I work all week long to put food on the table and now you're telling me I can't even go have a relaxing game of golf with my best friend?"

"Stop being so patronizing, I didn't say that. You're twisting my words. We don't have to go, I just thought it would be nice to go to the river. We haven't been in two years!" I could feel the ground start to crumble underneath me, what was I thinking? I was being too brave.

"Why are you so goddamn selfish all the time? I'm going golfing and you are staying here and that's the end of it! You are the one who wanted me to take this job so you can deal with it!"

"Oh, so now it's my fault?" I was furious that this had somehow turned into me holding him back when all I wanted to do was have some fun at the river like we used to. I couldn't let go of it. "What about you? You used to want to be with me, we had fun and now it's just cooking and cleaning and working – well I'm sick of it!" I threw a handful of clothes to the floor. I knew what was coming but it was too late. The shoes in his hand swung around full force and landed on the left side of my face. My head whipped around and I lost my balance falling into the closet door.

"You do *not* talk to me in that tone."

My entire body went numb. I was moving and speaking but I wasn't there. I remember a burning sensation where the sole of the shoe connected with my cheekbone and a splitting headache hit me that is still lingering as I pull out of the grocery parking lot. He helped me to my feet, which was almost as bad as the previous blow to my face. I started to feel dizzy and sick to my stomach.

"You okay? I'm sorry. You just didn't understand me. Everything's fine right?"

"Sure, I'm great." I said sarcastically.

"Listen, I gotta go meet Jason in town in 15 minutes. If I don't leave now, I'll be late." He walked into the bathroom and straightened his polo then quickly put his shoes on.

"Yeah."

"So, are we still gonna have your delicious homemade lasagna for dinner? I'll be home around seven or seven thirty."

"Yeah." I still couldn't think clearly. How was I supposed to discuss dinner after getting sideswiped by the shoes now on his feet? Fuck your homemade lasagna and fuck you.

"Alright sweetie." He grabbed a water bottle and his golf clubs and opened the door. "I'll see you later, love you."

I made eye contact and brought myself to nod, but could not speak actual words. *I*

17

love you, goodbye, have a great time. Nothing seemed to fit. All of the sudden everything around me started falling inward and I couldn't catch my breath. I ran down the stairs, half tripping and groping for the banister. I opened the back door and ran outside falling onto the dry grass, the tears coming now, uncontrollably. The numbness was wearing off and I was starting to feel the physical pain on my face, then the pain welling up from deep inside. Everything washed over me at once. All the moments of frustration, the cooking, the cleaning, the fights, and even the beautiful moments between us all became one big knot in the pit of my stomach. I felt as if I was completely alone in the world, invisible, but everyone else around me was smiling and laughing as if everything were just fine. Right now, I can't think of a worse feeling.

I took my time driving back home from the store. I decided to take a small detour down some of the back roads, the only place I can go within spitting distance that even remotely reminds me of home, where I used to walk as a kid and later with Nicholas. I didn't even want to think about him right now but my heart didn't agree with me and despite my sight-seeing, he was right there in the corner of my mind and evidently the side of my face as well. I arrived home, sad from the drive down memory lane, the opposite effect I was going for. My arms were full of groceries when I heard the phone ring. I rushed inside, leaving the keys in the door and picked up the phone.

"Hello?"

"Hey Becca, it's Megan, what's goin' on?"

"Oh…hey." I was disappointed it wasn't Nicholas and then furious at my own disappointment.

I managed to set down the paper bags of groceries on the counter and on half of the stove. I hate this kitchen; there is never enough counter space to do much of anything.

"I just walked in the door from doing some grocery shopping." *Oh yeah, the keys.*

"Oh yes, gotta love that. What are you having for dinner tonight?"

That was a good question. It was supposed to be lasagna but I wasn't sure if I felt like cooking it since he would be expecting me to. Just to spite him, I was thinking of having a bowl of cereal. The look on his face would be priceless!

"Lasagna, I guess. I told Nicholas I would cook it but I'm kind of irritated at him right now."

"Your lasagna is somethin' special. Why, what happened? He just can't keep his mouth shut, can he?"

I didn't want to tell her everything because what I experienced this afternoon wasn't him; it was someone else. I did want to vent though and Megan was the only person I felt I could trust and confide in. She knew me better than I knew myself and I still didn't have any real friends in Denver despite being here for four years now.

"Well, everything was great this morning then he was leaving to go golfing and I asked him if he wanted to maybe go to the river instead. I don't know, I guess I shouldn't have asked – I mean he…" I was going to say that he had plans and had a right to be upset but I couldn't lie to Megan or to myself and why should I give him credit he didn't deserve anyway? He didn't have plans and nothing gave him the right to do what he did. I knew what was right deep inside but my strength seemed to be diminishing. I just couldn't hold on to it.

"Becca, I know what you were going to say and you're wrong. I don't know what happened but nothing is worth making you feel this way, especially golf, an unbearably boring sport! You were just asking him to spend some time with you. Nothing wrong with that."

She could always make me laugh. "I know. Anyway, he ended up going golfing and here I am putting groceries away. What are you up to?" Time to change the subject.

"Just running some errands, a little cleaning and then I think we are going to splurge and see a movie tonight. I am so tired of

19

driving so I'm looking forward to just relaxing for a couple of hours."

"I know what you mean, it seems like I'm either cleaning or running errands or cooking."

"I hear ya! Well Becca, I hate to rush but I'm trying to navigate through traffic and some asshole on a cell phone just about killed the guy in front of me."

"Okay."

"Listen, just remember you can do it by yourself okay, you don't need him. There is a distinct difference between need and want."

"Oh, I know. We're fine, I'm just having a frustrating day."

"Okay."

"Alright, well I'll talk to you later this week."

"Okay, call me if you need to, bye."

"Bye Megan."

I'm fine. We're fine. Everything's okay.

7 - Eveline

"Kelly, why don't you come up to the board and underline the prepositions in all four sentences." She's a smart kid but obviously doesn't give herself enough credit. She hangs out with the wrong crowd, people who don't care what they look like and stand across the street from the Big Sky High School parking lot and smoke their cigarettes.

"Good, except for sentence number three. *My cat climbs under and over the fence.* Under and over are *both* prepositions since they both refer to the fence." Kelly nodded at me and looked at the ground before she took her seat.

"Alright class, that's it for today, remember to work on your midterm essays due in two weeks and find a newspaper article about an influential person in literature." The bell rings for the last time today and all the kids groan at their homework assignment and shuffle out the door. I sit down at my desk and sigh thinking about all that needs to be done.

I've been an English teacher for 16 years and I still love what I do. Education is so important; I guess that's why I couldn't just stop at a Bachelor's degree like a lot of the teachers I know. After getting divorced, I went back to school and received my Masters, then my PhD. I couldn't ask for a better career. I always knew I wanted to be a teacher, to be able to have a part in molding the adults of the future into what they should be. I love seeing them grow and change throughout high school. I am lucky enough to teach juniors and seniors when they begin to care about education and they start to think about more than just their social life. Teaching is also the one thing in my life that seems to have gone well, the one thing I have been really truly good at. I could always picture what I should be doing in my personal life, how I should act, who I should be as a wife and a mother but it just never worked out that way.

I finished grading the last of the papers for my third period class and packed up my stuff for the day. Usually, I stay until about 4 or 4:30 every day but my parents are coming in to town next weekend and there is so much I need to do to prepare. I glanced down at the photo on my desk as I turned out the lights. It has been five months since I've seen my daughter. Rebecca is the one other thing that somehow, I must have done right. She is beautiful and the most genuine and loving person I have ever known. Certainly, she is more like her dad, though I hate to admit it.

8 - Rebecca

I pulled down the oven door and chimed in with its creaking as if it were a song. What I wouldn't give for newer appliances! Ugh... The lasagna looks delicious. I *am* a good cook, aren't I?! I set it on the stove to cool and prepare the rest of the dinner I had planned while sneaking a peak at the corny *Lifetime* movie that was playing. Nicholas would have made fun of me if he were here then grabbed the remote and found some unbearably boring game of golf to watch. I don't know why he isn't a golf teacher or something instead of an architect. This afternoon's incident was still on my mind but fading fast with the anticipation of tonight being better. Nothing like a nice romantic dinner to fix all the problems in a relationship! He was probably just stressed out with work and why not – he does work all the time. I remember I used to want to be a pediatrician when I grew up. So much for that idea. I love kids and love helping people so I thought it would be a great combination. Sometimes I still think about it and try to work it out in my head. How could we afford it, maybe this, maybe that. Then after about thirty minutes I give up and resign myself to the fact that this is the path I chose and I will just have to deal with it. Damn practicality!

Nicholas always had a knack for building things. Throughout high school he would barely talk about anything else. He got what he wanted or as he would say "he worked for what he wanted". My opinion is somewhat different because I am the one who worked two, sometimes three jobs, nights, and weekends to help put him through school – *for us*. Back then it felt satisfying. It was so easy for me to put him first and it always made me happy to see him glow with pride at his accomplishments along the way and to know that I played a major role in his success. It's still easy for me to put him first. Is that my downfall? He's good at his job – I'll give him that. Finally, after three years of marriage and four years of hard work on both ends, it came time for his graduation. He was so excited he could barely contain himself and I was both happy for him and anticipating my decrease in workload. I couldn't wait to have what I had dreamed about for four years, a more *normal* life.

He graduated from the University of Colorado in Denver on May 8th. It was the most beautiful day and even better because we both had a strong sense of accomplishment although now that I look back on it, I'm not sure Nicholas noticed my pride and relief. Either way we were both happy. It was a good day at first. I wore a blue skirt with small, simple white flowers and a white linen shirt that flowed when the wind blew (my favorite feature). The graduation was outside in the stadium and white chairs were set up on the field in so many rows I lost count. I sat in the sixteenth row since the first ten rows were for the graduates. I had an aisle seat though, and I could see Nicholas clearly. His graduation cap and gown glowed slightly as the sun began its descent while his face beamed with pride and excitement. He stood just slightly on his tiptoes to catch my eye and gave me a wink and a grin. His name was finally called and he walked across the stage to accept his diploma. I clapped for him gave a loud "whoo-hoo" just for kicks. Inside I felt like I was going to burst with joy for him and what this milestone meant for him and for us.

Nicholas and I stayed around awhile longer after the ceremony ended to chat with his fellow classmates. He thanked them all for their support and help during the grueling four-year program and they all vowed to keep in touch and get together for a beer soon. I knew his friends relatively well and they were all very pleasant to me and included me in their conversations. The ride home was filled with promises of the perfect job, lots of money and a better life. I should have been happy at that moment but I felt unappreciated and forgotten. Maybe it was selfish of me to feel this way but all I really wanted to hear was recognition of all I had sacrificed for him and his accomplishments; just a few words of appreciation and understanding. It would have given me what I needed to forge ahead with the next stage of our lives. I wanted to know that he knew we were in it together. Instead of feeling happy I felt as if more had been taken from me than I had consented to, I felt empty.

Snapping back to reality, I stared at my gorgeous lasagna then at the clock – 7:00 – he should be home any minute. I walked away from the *Lifetime* movie and finished setting the table and thought, things will be different tonight.

9 - Nicholas

"You just name the time and place and I'll prove it!" I gave Jason a challenging shove.

"Whatever *golf master* – see you on the green next time around." Jason just thinks he's good at golf but as arrogant as it sounds, I just have a gift for it. I can't help it. I've loved the sport ever since I discovered my father hated it. *That sport is for men who don't have the guts for real sports like football!* He couldn't have been more wrong. Golf is a sport of intellect, patience and perseverance. It takes a calculating strategic mind to be good at it and though Jason has been my best friend since I was a kid, he doesn't have what it takes.

I started walking away from the Rocky Mountain Country Club toward my truck. It was an old Ford that I've had since I was a teenager and one that I hope to get rid of soon now that I have a good job. A brand-new Ford F250 will be mine as soon as I can make it happen. I grew up in an old house outside of Missoula and vowed that I would do better when it was my turn to support a family. I would have a nice truck, a nice house – a beautiful wife, the whole package. I have the wife, Rebecca. I stopped next to the truck, threw my clubs in the bed and pulled a pack of cigarettes from a hidden place under the driver's seat. Becca didn't like me to smoke but damn it, it sounded good right now. The day was warm and sunny with a warm breeze and just a few clouds. I leaned up against my truck and inhaled deeply. I took advantage of moments that I could just sit back and relax without someone breathing down my neck. Lately Becca has been getting on my nerves. I can't do anything right and no matter what I do nothing is good enough for her. She used to think the sun rose in my eyes and now I'm not so sure any more.

I thought back to this morning and felt a pang of guilt. I didn't mean to hurt her. She just doesn't listen; she just wouldn't let it go and I swear sometimes that's the only way she gets it. She is my saving grace though, and I can't help but need her in my life. She stuck by me while I went to school and she is so good to me. I'm hoping that eventually she'll get the hang of being my wife. We have only been married three years but it seems like we've just started our lives and I am anxious to have a child. I guess we both are, for different reasons. I just need her to know her place before we do. I was raised in an environment where my mother was what I hope Becca becomes. She put her husband and her kids first above everything and did everything without complaining. The cooking, cleaning and normal upkeep of daily life seemed to invigorate her while it drags Becca down.

I glanced at my watch *6:30 pm*. I should probably head home. With any luck Bec has made that delicious lasagna of hers. I just know tonight will give us a chance to be better. I will make up for this afternoon somehow. I took one last long drag of my cigarette and tossed it to the gravel at my feet. Just as I turned to go, I heard a truck drive up next to mine and come to a sliding halt. Tiny pellets of gravel sprayed the bed of my worn-out Ford and I turned to see some familiar faces.

"Hey! What's up man?" they called.

It was Aaron and Jenna, friends of mine from college. "Hey – hey! What brings you two up here? I was just about to take off."

"We ran into Jason down at the Exxon and he said we might be able to catch you up here. Thought you might want to grab a drink at Joe's Club. You down?"

I thought of Becca and her lasagna and then I thought of a nice cold beer, the smoky atmosphere and that comfortable feeling of everyone around you not worried about a damn thing. "Hell yeah, I'm down, I'll follow you there." A couple beers wouldn't hurt anything and I could make it home in time for dinner.

Jenna gave me a smile and a wink as they pulled out of the parking lot.

10 - Rebecca

A commercial came on and I snapped out of my TV trance and looked at the clock on the wall. Eight o'clock. My heart sank, I should have known he would do something like this. My throat started to ache and swell and my eyes began to water. *Don't let him do it, don't cry, don't let him win.* I took a deep breath and cut myself a piece of lasagna. Your mind runs wild when you don't have the answers. I tried to call him but the phone just rang until I heard his voicemail. I left a message trying not to sound too frantic just in case he was okay. I didn't want to sound like the nagging wife, but I was worried. He could have at least called me.

Dinner was delicious but my face was still burning and sore to the touch from this afternoon and I couldn't shake the nervousness. I was starting to feel very nauseous. I paced around the house, cleaning some more and finally went back to the television in a desperate attempt to distract my wandering mind. The episode of Law and Order ended and I glanced at the clock. 9:05 and no word from Nicholas. I dialed his cell phone again, tears starting to fall on my bruised swollen cheek. I reached his voicemail again and broke down neglecting to hang up the phone. I thought, how could I have hoped that he wouldn't let me down? I knelt on the floor in the middle of the living room with my head down. My hair was in my face and stuck to my hot tears. I cried from my heart, slow quiet tears then a deep sobbing began as I let myself fall apart and release all the emotion from this horrible horrible day.

11 - Nicholas

"I told you not to take that bet man! How many games of pool do you need to lose before you realize that I'm better than you? Pure talent right here Jase." The guys all slap me on the back in congratulations and laughed. Jenna and a couple of her friends are sitting on stools in the corner drinking and whispering about something.

"Three out of five man, just one more to win all my money back then we'll quit." Jason pleads.

"Alright, one more but I need a smoke. I'll be right back – go get us some more beer." I know it must be late and I needed a good excuse to call Becca. Before stepping outside, I turned back and caught Jenna's eye and winked. Outside the bar I breathed in the cool fresh air and lit up a cigarette visualizing Jenna's round face and blonde hair. I loved nights like this.

"Alright Bec, let's see how many messages you left." I dialed voicemail first to see how she sounded before I called her directly. I needed to prepare properly for my argument. The first message predictable – a little worried but she seemed fine. I heard the time of the second one, "Shit." I didn't think it was that late. The second message began to play. There was no sound at first, then all of the sudden everything went blurry around me. The sound echoing from my cell phone wasn't Becca. It was pure, desperate sadness – a moaning and sobbing weighted with pain and so many emotions I wasn't sure how to react. That couldn't be Becca, there was no message just sobbing until I heard 'end of message – beep'. I knew I had to get the hell out of here.

I popped my head back in the bar, "Gotta go guys. I'm callin' it a night. See ya tomorrow!" I heard '*Awww, c'mon*' from the guys in the background as I walked out.

Shit, what did I do?

29

12 - Rebecca

I woke up on the living room floor to the distinctive sound of Nicholas's old truck pulling into the driveway. I sat upright and took in my surroundings. Lasagna was still on the table with my dinner plate on the counter, a place still set for Nicholas and the television on mute. I shook my head and rubbed my face to wake up checking the time 10:16. Interesting. I rushed to the kitchen trying to clean up what I could before he came inside. I could hear the truck come to a stop and the engine go quiet. I remembered my sobbing into the phone and what his voicemail must have sounded like and felt an immense embarrassment. I moved the phone from the living room floor to the counter, dimmed the lights and ran upstairs. I could hear the garage door open and close and his key in the door.

I put on my favorite flannel Snoopy pajamas bottoms and a white t-shirt and jumped into bed. It was a little early for bed but I still didn't feel well and thought what the hell. I could think of a thousand reasons I didn't want to face him. I was embarrassed at my phone message and at my own concern, angry at his insensitivity and lack of concern for someone other than himself, and I hated being put in the position where I almost felt like a parent. I am his wife for God's sake, not his mother! No words could be spoken between us that would make me feel okay or make him sorry for his actions. It's best that we call this day shot to hell and end it before it gets worse. The wall I faced from my side of the bed had a glow from the light in the hall. I was frozen and listening to every sound. I could almost picture him as he entered the house and put his keys on the table seeing the covered lasagna and the unused place setting that was intended for him. He mumbled something that sounded like *oh shit*. Maybe he would feel guiltier with me being in bed already – I could hope for that small selfish miracle.

13 - Nicholas

The empty place setting and what had to be covered lasagna spoke volumes. It's amazing how emptiness can take up so much room. I breathed in deeply and sighed knowing that she must be asleep. I was thankful that I didn't have to face her. I was disappointed in myself for losing track of time, for choosing so many things over her, and for not seeing her anguish. As I stood there and envisioned how her evening must have gone, I began to experience an unexpected emotion, a defensive anger seeping through my embarrassment. Why should I have to answer to her anyway? I suppose I should have at least called and let her know I wasn't going to be there for dinner – I'll give her that. I knew what I had to do. I learned early in our relationship that it didn't take much to get Becca to forgive me.

From the beginning I wanted her, she was beautiful, confident and shy all at once and she had a peculiar ability to surprise me. A lot of girls are predictable and she never was. I loved that about her. I knew as we started dating that she loved me more than I loved her. It's not like I don't love her. I've never cared for anyone the way I love Becca. It's just that there's a difference in our affection and the way we respond to each other. I'm her weakness and I know she would do anything for me. She would say 'you're not just my husband, you're my best friend' and although I nod and smile and kiss her beautiful lips, I see those roles as two very separate people. I tell Jason very different things than I would share with Becca and I consider him my best friend. Becca is my wife, not my best friend. Knowing this about us, I suppose I do take advantage of her forgiving nature. I know exactly what I need to do to get on her good side again and it always works. Sometimes I get so sick and tired of catering to this characteristic. Why can't we just skip the '*I'm sorry, you know I love you*' crap? She should know all that by now shouldn't she? Why must I repeat myself if it's understood?

I climbed the stairs to our bedroom and saw her silhouette under the covers facing the wall. The light from the hallway fell across the bed and made the wall glow gold. I knelt in the middle of the bed and bent my head close to her face. I kissed her cheek and whispered in her ear even though she was asleep.

"I'm sorry Bec, I should've called you. I'll make it up to you." I sat there for a moment secretly hoping for a response, preferably a positive response, maybe even to get laid but that was pushing it I suppose. "Love you."

I closed the bedroom door behind me and headed back down the stairs. I grabbed the remote and settled in to my favorite chair with some lasagna.

14 - Rebecca

I heard his apology loud and clear but I just couldn't bring myself to give in just yet. As crazy as it sounds, I wanted to. I wanted to be held, consoled, and told that everything would be okay. I wanted to fall apart in his arms and for him to be *my* strength for once. He kissed my left cheek and I winced – a reminder of the pain he caused earlier in this mess of a day. He closed the door and left the room eerily quiet. What do you do when the person who hurts you is the same person you want to save you?

It was almost a week later that I woke up with only one thing on my mind. So much can change in such a short period of time. Nicholas had left for work and now was my opportunity to find out for sure. Somehow, I already knew the truth but I needed to see it for myself. I paced as I waited for what seemed like an eternity for the appearance of two pink lines. I checked the instructions...positive. I checked again, sure that it must be a mistake, maybe two lines meant negative. I read it slowly. *I can't believe I'm pregnant.* I steadied myself and sat down on the toilet seat feeling a little light headed and nauseous. What am I going to do?

On shaky legs, I stood up slowly and walked over to the bathroom mirror looking at the woman on the other side. Her face flushed and a transparent green and blue bruise on the left from his brilliant 'golf swing' to the side of my head last week. I brought my hand up and touched my cheek and instinctively brought my other hand to my stomach, remembering. I smiled and said out loud with as much confidence as I could muster, "things will be better now," almost believing myself.

15 - Megan

"You're pregnant!" I just couldn't believe my ears. Why do things like this always happen at the most inopportune time, or in Becca's case any time she was married to Nick would be a bad time. She is nowhere near ready for this. Then again maybe this is the one thing that will save her. I decided then and there to be as supportive as I could, given the circumstances.

"I know," Rebecca says in between sobs, "what am I gonna do? I just got a promotion at work and I don't even know how Nicholas will react!" She is starting to lose control.

"Becca, listen to me. Everything will be fine. You're gonna have a baby! Congratulations!" I can't believe what I'm about to say but I know it must be said. "Nick will be fine – are you kidding? You know he's always wanted kids, both of you have. It might not have been exactly planned but you guys were gonna try eventually and maybe… maybe it will clue him in a little to what is important." I was reaching there; everyone knows having kids never fixes a relationship, but I knew Rebecca would want it to and we both knew deep down that it was her only shot at reaching Nicholas. If this doesn't change him, nothing will.

"You think so?" she sniffed, a glimmer of hope in her voice that something might actually work out for the best.

"Of course I do."

"How do I tell Nicholas? What do I say?"

I didn't know the first thing about this, we don't have kids and had no immediate plans for it, but I imagined what might be best in her situation, given Nicholas's quick temper. "Well, I know you're not going to be able to contain yourself for a whole 24 hours so you might as well tell him at dinner tonight. What are you cooking?"

"I have the day off today so I'm making chicken with a cream sauce, steamed vegetables and garlic rice."

"Wow! You should really go into catering or something, you're amazing. Jeff is lucky if I cook some pork chops on the grill or something! I'm serious about catering by the way. Okay let's focus…so you set the table with a couple of candles and have dinner all ready then just as you both sit down to eat you tell him before he can open his mouth and ruin dinner."

"Whatever Megan. That sounds good though, I guess you have a point. That way we can talk about it a little through dinner, I'm starting to think he might even be a little excited about it."

She started to tear up again but it was a different kind of crying. "Megan, I don't know what I'd do without you."

"Oh, I don't know, you'd be free of my pestering – "

"No, you're my best friend and you've always been there for me, knowing just what to say. I just – I just want to thank you, that's all."

As trying as Rebecca can be, I love her and we understand and accept each other as is. "No problem, any time. I'm so happy for you Becca and I hope things get better for you guys. You deserve it!" A comfortable silence fell on the conversation, "So! When should we go baby shopping? I have to make a trip out there!"

"Megan really? That would be wonderful! I would love that; it's been too long since we've seen each other. After I talk to Nicholas, I'll let you know okay?"

"Sounds good. All right, well I'll let you get things together; let me know how it goes. Good luck!"

"Thanks, Megan."

She sounded happier and excited and I felt that she now had a purpose. Maybe it's possible that this baby is a blessing in disguise, maybe she could be happy. Maybe *they* could be happy.

16 - Eveline

It was good to talk to Rebecca. I had a half-day today so I got home just as I would normally be leaving work. She left a message on the answering machine and she sounded so full of life it took me by surprise. I set my bag on the floor by the desk and played it again just to hear her voice. I was thinking how it was a little strange for me to be surprised that she sounded happy. Was I missing something in her life? Had she been unhappy before this? I've been so busy with school, preparing for a big presentation I have coming up on character and behavioral education, not to mention my parents coming into town this weekend – which should be interesting. I must have missed something.

I told myself *don't be so hard on yourself, maybe she is just extra happy about something in particular.* Yes, that was it. I called her back as I started to make myself dinner. She was pregnant! Throughout the conversation I discovered that she had already called Megan and her dad but she was just about to tell Nicholas at dinner so she couldn't talk long. I told her how elated I was for her and how happy I was to finally have a grandchild! I told her I would get a gift pack together for her and the baby and send it before the weekend.

"Mom, you don't have to do that there's plenty of time."

"Well, I don't care, I'll go tomorrow after work, there is so much you'll need so just leave it me okay? Don't worry, I won't get everything, just a few odds and ends that every mother should have." She tried to squeeze as many thoughts and happenings into a sentence as she could. She seemed eager to share her joy and anxiety. I remember feeling the same way.

"Thanks. So, are you anxious about your parents coming into town?"

"Oh, a little but you know how they are, I think it will be their last trip away from home and I want them to have a good time. It will be just fine. I've got lots of things planned including a little relaxing time so don't worry. You just take care of that baby!"

"I will mom, well, I'll keep you posted on things and give me a call sometime this weekend."

"Well, honey I'll give you a call when they leave and to make sure you got the package, okay?"

"Alright mom, well, I have to go. Dinner is all ready and I think I just heard Nicholas's truck pull up."

"Okay, I love you Rebecca, I'm so proud of you!" God, I love her. I know she will understand a mother's love as soon as she sees that little face look back at her and depend on her for everything. I may have had my moments, but never did a day go by when I didn't love her and want the best for her. Even when she was a teenager and I could have slapped her she made me so angry. I still loved her.

Wow, I'm a grandmother. That will be some good news to share with my parents when they come, something for us to talk about. My parents and I have had a rocky and mostly ugly history. I have two brothers that chose to live the life that my parents wanted us all to live. I was the rebel who left Massachusetts and moved to Montana to start a new life in the west; the life they didn't approve of. This rebellion combined with the fact that I was always a burden as a child made it difficult for me to feel that they ever truly loved me. We have gotten in horrible fights and have also had really wonderful times together that I wouldn't trade for the world. I guess that's the story of any family, but I always felt like there was a piece of me missing without their approval. Hence, my constant need to mend things with them. They are good people, especially my dad and as I get older, I realize how important it is to let go of things that happened in the past.

17 - Rebecca

After talking to Megan, I felt like this baby could be more of a blessing instead of a burden. I had a purpose now, this small life inside me tugging at my heart. I started to get the house cleaned up and the ingredients out for dinner. As I performed these tasks that now came second nature to me, I thought about what Megan said. Catering huh? Not a bad idea really, I *am* a good cook and I'm always trying out different things. I wonder if I could actually do it, my own catering business! As I wiped off the table, I noticed I was smiling and then how foreign it was to be smiling as I was cleaning. I moved on to the living room picking up random items that found their way to the floor and the couch cushions. I allowed myself to imagine what it would be like.

I imagined myself in an apron behind a table and employees around me that I instructed on what to do next. There is a beautiful spread of dishes that I have prepared for a wedding including a beautiful cake with four tiers and a trail of ribbon frosting around each layer. Then I imagined Nicholas dropping by with the baby in his arms waving her little hand at me. I almost saw her face but I shook myself free of my fantasy world. Maybe someday I could make it all come true.

I cleaned all morning then drove to the store to pick up a few candles and a little box. I decided that I would put the pregnancy test in a small box and put a ribbon around it. I'm not usually that creative but it came to me as I was shopping; besides it would save me from having to say the actual words right away. After lunch and a mid-afternoon episode of Law and Order, I began cooking what I would come to remember as the 'Guess What I'm Pregnant' meal. I kind of giggled to myself when this occurred to me. I checked the clock in the kitchen, Nicholas should be home in about ten minutes or so and the garlic rice was almost done. The phone rang and it was mom! I hadn't heard from her in a while and I *was* hoping she would call before Nicholas came home.

"Mom! It's so good to hear from you!"

"Well, honey I just got home from work and I got your message, you sound different…good different though. How is everything?"

"You're never going to believe this, I'm pregnant!" I was shocked at how the words just spilled from my mouth. I thought it would be more difficult to tell people, especially my mother, as I wasn't really sure about how well she liked Nicholas. No one really knew him like I did since we live so far from everyone in my family. Dad had received the news with obvious apprehension although he did his best not to show it. You could tell it was one of those responses where the other person wasn't sure if you were happy about the pregnancy or not and therefore were not sure what their emotion should be. Why can't people just be honest?

"Wow sweetie, oh my goodness! Congratulations! How far along are you?"

"I have no idea. I just took a pregnancy test this morning. I'll make an appointment to go in soon. I actually haven't even told Nicholas yet. He should be coming home in a few minutes so I can't talk long. I thought I would tell him at dinner, what do you think?"

"I think that's a good idea."

We talked for a few more minutes, then I heard his truck pull into the driveway and said my goodbyes. I looked at the door and put my hand to my stomach and breathed in, slow and deep. All of the sudden I was so nervous I felt nauseous and a little shaky. I lit the candles and busied myself bringing the chicken from the stove to the table as Nicholas walked in the door. He was dressed in his tan slacks and an olive-green polo, which made his shoulders appear larger and his beer-belly smaller. In the candlelight he was more attractive than I have seen him look in a long time. He looked astonished and a little confused but a crooked smile broke across his face and I looked away to hide my prideful grin.

"Wow." He said, setting his bag and keys on the small table in the entryway. I have been trying to get him to set his stuff there for a year instead of on the table; and now, when he is most distracted, he actually does it. Amazing. He walked toward me still

39

dumbfounded but readily accepting the display of food and candles.

"Yeah, I just thought it would be nice you know…we haven't done this in a while so." I trailed off and finished putting the vegetables and rice on the table along with some homemade dinner rolls I decided to do at the last minute.

"Bec, this looks great. You're amazing, have I ever told you how amazing you are?!"

"Well, I am always open to hearing *that*!" I joked and laughed a little – a more nervous laugh than I intended but I don't think he caught it. "Are you hungry?"

"Am I hungry? Hell yes, I'm hungry!" He still had a huge grin on his face and I couldn't help but make fun of him for it.

"It's not like I never cook, you look so shocked." I tried to play it down a little, more to ease my nerves than to throw him off. I definitely won't be able to get through dinner. I have to tell him before dinner as casually as possible.

"Well, I know Bec but this is – well, it's just nice that's all. Shall we?" He motioned for us to sit and I started dishing out each part of the meal.

When our plates were full and we sat staring at each other smiling – it occurred to me that the moment was just right and maybe this really would work out after all.

"Oh!" I said as if I had just remembered something. "I almost forgot; this is for you." I pulled out the slim white jewelry box with a white ribbon wrapped around it. I slid it next to his plate, my hand just slightly trembling. He looked at the box and looked up at me.

"Becca, what's this?"

"Open it." I didn't have it in me to give him any more information. I thought I would just burst at the seams if I had to wait any longer. What would he say? What would he think?

"Alright." He pulled at the ribbon and opened the box. "What? Oh, Becca."

"Yep. It's positive, I – I just found out this morning."

"Oh my God Becca! Are you sure?" He jumped up so fast from the table it startled me and I pushed my chair back. "This is amazing, we're having a baby?" He rushed toward me and scooped me up into his arms and twirled me into the kitchen.

I was trembling with relief and I started to cry tears of pure happiness. Just to see how happy he was made everything fit together. I screamed and cried and we kissed; a passionate hungry kiss that seemed to replace all the words necessary to describe the moment. It went better than I could have imagined. I started to feel a little nauseous and he must have noticed because he stopped twirling me.

"Oh, I'm sorry, you okay?"

"Oh, I'm fine, just a little nauseous that's all."

He stopped and cupped my face in his hands. "I love you Rebecca and I'm so happy. I just can't believe it."

"I love you to. I was so nervous about telling you, but I wanted it to be special so that's why I made the dinner. I'm so glad you're happy. A baby! Can you believe it?"

"I know. I guess this is the 'Guess What I'm Pregnant' meal then." We started to sit down at the dinner table and started giggling and then we both broke out in a fit of laughter. I could barely breathe I was laughing so hard, but in between breaths I told him that I thought the exact same thing earlier as I was cooking. This just made us laugh harder until we were both on the floor in the fetal position. Finally, we caught our breaths and looked over at each other from the dining room floor.

"I guess we should eat before it gets cold huh?"

"Yeah, I wouldn't want your beautiful meal to go to waste."

I smiled at him and I finally felt a sense of peace.

18 - Nicholas

It was short notice so I couldn't make it to Becca's first doctor's appointment but she found out she was nine weeks pregnant. The doctor also gave her a bunch of other information about eating, exercising and general preparation information. My life began to be dictated in weeks instead of days and months, which was foreign to me and was taking some getting used to like everything else. Seems like yesterday she was telling me the news and here we are 5 months or – 20 weeks - later at her first ultrasound appointment where they say we'll be able to see the baby. I just can't imagine it. Up until now it hasn't seemed real. She started showing a little about a month ago but other than that nothing is different for me.

Work and life have continued on except, there is something different between us, something better. We haven't had a fight since she found out she was pregnant and she's just been a different person, not to mention the sex! She's taken on a more domestic role while at the same time working steadily as she did before without a complaint. Becca even looks happier and more at peace than I have ever seen her look before, making her even more attractive. Becca says we should be able to hear the heart beat and maybe even find out if the baby is a boy or a girl. I requested to leave work early as soon as I knew the date and time of the appointment, I could barely wait another day and it's finally here.

19 - Eveline

"Okay Mom, I'll pick you and Dad up from the airport tomorrow morning. Eight-thirty, I know, me too. Have a good flight, love you."

There is an inexplicable emotion that always remains between a child and her parents no matter what atrocities take place. Though I have hated them at times, more specifically my mother, I find myself in desperate need of their approval and adoration. For years I tried to get out from underneath their judgment and now I need them. Here I am 47 years old and I still need to know that they're proud of me. You would think I would have grown out of that by now, but it still lingers. We have had a good relationship for the past year or so and I've even traveled up to see them; it was a surprisingly enjoyable visit. I'm anxious for them to see my life as a successful teacher in a good school and in my own house. Their only disappointment in me is probably that I didn't marry into money and that I'm not married now. I can't let that bother me though, I've done all I can in that department and maybe I'll just have to accept the fact that I might not be good at marriage or love for that matter. I've been good at most things in my life but relationships seem to be my nemesis. All relationships except for my relationship with Rebecca. I feel like she understands and accepts me, not only as a mother, but also as a woman.

Tomorrow morning I'll pick them up at the airport. Anticipating my nervousness, I have everything planned, even time for them to rest. I know that Mom has been struggling lately and Dad gets a little confused sometimes so I need to try and remember that they are not what they used to be. I hate to admit it, I suppose it is selfish of me, but I am almost thankful that I don't live close to them. My brothers are the ones taking care of them, checking on them and handling things that are too consuming for them at their age. It is a confusing, terrible thing to have to watch your parents age to a point where you almost don't recognize them anymore. Since I don't see them that often, I am a little nervous about what it will be like. Well, I can't think about it now, so much to do tonight before they come. I grabbed the garbage from the upstairs bathroom and started down the stairs. I stopped mid-way to look at the photos along the wall as I often do. Just then I realized I didn't have any photos of my parents or brothers on the wall. I just hadn't had a chance to hang them yet (even though they've been in a box for almost a year).

I rushed down the stairs and put the garbage in the garage and walked over to the toolbox. I'm not a very handy person, that was my ex-husband's thing but I do have the necessities – a hammer, screwdriver, nails, and a tape measure - I think. I grabbed the hammer and small nails. It took longer than I intended but I managed to find some photos and replace some of Rebecca and friends with Mom and Dad. I was famished by the time I finished and put the hammer in a very cramped "everything drawer" in the kitchen. Everyone has one of these; a drawer that collects random things that you need but rarely use, a AAA battery, matches, markers, and different kinds of tape. Finally, by nine o' clock I was sitting at my little kitchen table with a glass of wine and a chicken pot pie, satisfied with the house and ready for tomorrow. I said out loud to the walls, "Here we go."

20 - Rebecca

"Wasn't that amazing! It's a real person – a girl, fingers and toes and a heartbeat." I tried not to be too overly excited but I was secretly hoping for a girl and it *was* a girl. I knew Nicholas would be disappointed but would try not to show it. He says it doesn't matter to him but he has made comments before and every time he talks about the baby, he has referred to it as a boy. When we found out the baby was a girl, I looked at him and saw a fleeting moment of displeasure before he caught my glance and gave me a giant cheesy grin.

"I know. It's a girl, wow."

"The heart beat was strong too so that's good, everything is looking good."

"Yep, everything's right on track." His tone was upbeat and had that sound of attempted interest, but really, he was thinking about something else.

I rubbed my growing belly and leaned my head against the passenger window. "I wish Mom could be here, I wish I could talk to her. I still feel like I'm in shock, like I'm part of a movie or something. It just doesn't even seem real."

Nicholas put his hand on my leg to console me, "I know honey, I'm sorry."

It was the weekend after I found out I was pregnant. Mom's parents came to visit and she had picked them up Saturday morning but I promised her I wouldn't call because she just gets so stressed out. I had a feeling I should call to see how things were going but I didn't want to make it harder for her. Sunday evening, I was cooking dinner and the phone rang.

"Hello?"

"Hi, is Rebecca there?"

"This is her. Who is this?" I usually recognize everyone that calls because the only people that call me is family, work, or Megan. At first, I thought it could be a solicitor – they always seem to call during dinner – but there was a sad urgency to the voice.

"Rebecca, hi, its James, your mom's older brother." There was a brief silence.

"James, hi, it's been quite a while since I talked to you. Is everything okay?" He has never called me before. The only time we have communicated is during a visit with Mom when she was with her family in Boston or through Christmas cards. Something wasn't right.

"Rebecca, I have some bad news about your Mom. I'm in Missoula and your mom is in jail right now until things can be straightened out."

He spoke in a calm tone but he seemed out of sorts. I knew if he was already in Missoula it must be bad. I reached for a kitchen chair and sank into it. Nicholas looked over his shoulder from the living room and caught my eye. He did a double take and mouthed *are you okay?* I wasn't quite sure yet so I just nodded slightly.

"What happened? Is she okay?"

"Your mom hurt Nana pretty bad. She hit her with a hammer." All the blood seemed to have left my body and I felt dizzy. James took a deep breath and continued, "Nana has been taken to the hospital and Granddad is here with me. I already went to the hospital and Nana is in surgery right now. The doctor said she'll be in recovery for a while so I thought I would come back here." He paused to collect himself and he must have pulled the phone away from himself but I could still hear him crying. "I – I'm on my way over to the jail now to talk to your mom and to the police about what happened."

"James, I don't understand, what happened? They came to visit her yesterday; everything was fine." I started crying out of pure frustration and fear of what I was about to hear.

James told me pieces of what had happened early that morning and promised he would keep in touch. I hung up with him, stunned.

The next few weeks were a blur. It's amazing how something wonderful and something horrible can be happening at the same time. I had found out that I was pregnant and days later my mother commits this horrible act. I was really confused about what had really happened that morning and still couldn't understand. She was educated, intelligent, teacher of the year and a truly good person. People like that don't snap – do they? If it was true, then I wondered about my own behavior and what I would be like as a mom. Was the lack of tolerance and control genetic? I only allowed myself to ponder these questions for a moment or two before I dismissed them…temporarily. Mom was in jail for a few days then released on bail while the investigation continued. She called me after returning to her house, which had to be trying in and of itself. She was a complete wreck.

She spoke between tears in each conversation and her emotions ranged from deep sadness and distress to a frightening positivity that didn't make any sense. After about a week she decided to tell me the whole story about what occurred that August morning. I didn't dare ask the question, for fear that the situation would become more real and that she would simply fall to pieces and disappear and I had a feeling she needed me as much as I needed her.

21 - Eveline

We were discussing the baby and her upcoming appointment and avoiding the elephant in the room, when I couldn't bare it any longer. Rebecca should know and I couldn't keep it inside for another minute. The events of August 12th were haunting every moment of each day and I thought that maybe, if I shared it with Rebecca, I could release some of the burden. I had now lost everything that I had worked my whole life for, my job as a teacher in a great school, friends, home and probably my family. I guess on some level I also thought that maybe she would understand me when I couldn't make sense of myself. She has always been more compassionate than me. I was reaching out for help from my own daughter and at the same time, so ashamed of myself that I wasn't sure I could get through what I was about to say. This would be my last chance.

"Rebecca," my voice cracked and became almost a whisper.

"Mom, are you okay?"

"I'm only going to tell you this once and then I have to go. Just let me talk or I don't think I can make it through this okay?" I had recounted the events of that morning a thousand times in my head but hadn't said it out loud since I was arrested and questioned.

"I picked up my parents at the airport and they seemed happy to see me. Mom complained about the plane ride and she looked much older than I remembered from last year's visit. I had planned everything so they would have fun but be able to relax too. The first day went really well but I had no idea how much help they needed. I just – I just wasn't prepared for how much assistance they needed, especially Mom." I had to stop to regain my composure. Just picturing her brought so much pain and disbelief, I still couldn't believe I was living in this nightmare of a life. Rebecca was dutifully silent.

"Anyway, the next morning, Sunday we had all woken up early and I helped Mom get dressed, cleaned up and to use the bathroom. Dad started his shower and Mom and I were going down the stairs to get some tea. She said she would like some. She was walking in front of me and about half way down she tripped or something, I'm not really sure what happened." My voice was cracking and I was crying. I wasn't even sure Rebecca could hear me. I know I must have been practically whispering but everything felt so loud and overwhelming in my head. It was as if I didn't even want to utter the words.

"I reached out to catch her, to stop her from falling but I didn't grab her in time. She fell forward down the stairs and lay sprawled at the bottom of the stairs screaming. I ran down to help her and to tell her it would be okay. She must have been really confused, she kept screaming at me and calling me a bitch. She told me to get away from her and leave her alone. I tried to calm her down but she grabbed the flesh on my arm and twisted until it burned while she continued to yell at me and call me names. She started screaming at me like when I was a child." I had to pause again, if I could just get through this then I could move on and this will all become the past. "All of the sudden I felt myself fall through time. People say in some moments, their 'life flashes before their eyes', well it was something like that. All the moments I was sad, lonely, beaten and abandoned because of her, flashed through my mind like a timeline of memories."

Rebecca was starting to cry now but trying to hold it back the best she could. I couldn't even bare to comfort her. "I wrenched my body away from hers. She was trying to get up... clawing at me. I glanced over by the wall and saw the hammer I had left by the wall from the night before my parents had arrived. I had been replacing some pictures on the wall of friends with pictures of them and other family. I wanted them to see I had their pictures on the wall, you know, that they were a part of my life." I broke down sobbing and curled myself up into the smallest position possible just to feel close to something, what happened next was burned into my soul and I saw it before I could speak the words.

"I grabbed the hammer and hit her in the head, a few times, I guess. She was screaming so loud. I kept telling her to shut up, to be quiet, I just couldn't think. I went to the kitchen and got a garbage bag."

"Mom…" Rebecca gasped in a hushed tone. I could almost hear her tears.

"I couldn't get her to be quiet. I shoved the garbage bag in her mouth and took the hammer to the sink and washed it off. I went to hide it in the garage and then I realized what was happening. I thought *what am I doing?* I ran to my cell phone and called 911 and told them everything. I ran across the street to the neighbor's house for help. I was hysterical and I – I'm so sorry!" My emotions were out of my control now. I was reeling with shame, anger, disbelief and sadness all at once.

"I have to go now. I love you." I hung up not caring what I left behind and with nothing left to give.

22 - Rebecca

Between the phone call and the time Mom was sentenced, it was a roller coaster ride of emotions and indecision. She finalized the sale of her house and most of her belongings; she gave things to me that I couldn't refuse for fear of pushing her over the edge emotionally. She rented an apartment but shortly after, was convinced by friends that she couldn't live on her own right now. I had nightmares that she had committed suicide and often woke up in the middle of the night screaming. Nicholas was there most of the time, except for nights he was playing pool, and comforted me to the best of his ability. Some nights I walked downstairs in my nightgown and would kneel at the window where I could see the moon and pray for her. I'm not really sure I believe in God, if there is a God, I haven't seen much good come from Him and from praying to Him for that matter, but I had to try.

Since the night that James called and told me the news about what Mom had done, I now jump every time the phone rings. The ring became a sound that caused my senses to heighten and every muscle in my body to tense, ready for the next blow. The only good thing about that time in my life was that Nicholas and I were close, we rarely argued and he was more attentive than I have ever seen him. What was feared most by myself, and I would imagine her entire family, happened. This is what tipped the scale and moved the course of Mom's life from a trial to a sentence.

I picked up the phone, "James?" I just knew it was him.

"Rebecca. I've got some bad news, its Nana. She's gone. There was too much blood in her brain and…" He stopped and I could tell he was holding back tears and a flood of emotion. How hard it must be to be the one that has to be strong for everyone else. I began to cry myself and I barely knew her.

"James, I'm so sorry. I'm so sorry." What else could I say, my mother had killed his mother – their mother. Her passing away gave the circumstances a whole new weight. "James, if there's anything I can do, please let me know okay?"

"Yes, thank you. I have some things to take care of but I'll keep in touch. I know we would love for you to come up for the funeral if you can. But, well, there's so much going on, I'll call you soon okay?"

"Okay James, good bye." He sounded so overwhelmed. I hung up the phone and felt nauseous. I was only about 13 weeks pregnant at the time and still experiencing morning sickness. This whole scenario wasn't helping my stress level or my state of mind. I could only hope that it wasn't affecting the baby.

I called Megan and Dad to let them know what was going on and to get some support. I wasn't sure what I needed, but it helped to talk about it. In the midst of my confusion and sadness I couldn't help but feel heavy from all the sadness around me. It was as if I could see each person's experiences through their eyes and there was nothing but regret. Mom was filled with regret to the point of it becoming mentally debilitating, Granddad had now lost his wife of 65 years at the hands of his youngest daughter, James and his brother had lost a mother at the hands of their sister. Then I realized, here I was, in the middle of it all, the daughter of a murderer. That is what the crime would be considered now – murder. Nana had died within a month of the crime.

The next day, Mom called me to say her final goodbyes, she said the police would be coming soon to arrest her.

"I've decided to plead guilty," she said in a shaky voice, "I can't go to trial, I don't think I could make it through. I tried to tell them about the abuse I went through as a kid and that's why I think I flipped out but I just can't go through a trial. It's in God's hands now."

I couldn't believe what I was hearing. In God's hands? I didn't dare convey my conflicting emotions to her but I thought to myself, you took it out of God's hands when you hit her with a hammer don't you think?! Now you are depending on God to save you? I knew, however that she was right, she couldn't emotionally handle a trial. I think if she could have gone through a trial, she might have been able to get a reduced sentence by bringing out the alleged abuse. Everyone has their own shit to go through, their own crappy childhood, why should she be any different? Plenty of people experience abuse, abandonment and worse and they don't kill anyone. She was just never able to let it go.

"I know Mom. I can't believe any of this is happening."

"Rebecca, I want you to know that I love you so much. Take care of yourself."

"I will Mom."

"You know you can write me! It will be a little while before I can write you with the address but I will okay? Will you write me?" She was crying now.

"Of course I will. I'll write you all the time." *Why is this happening?*

"Okay, honey, I gotta go, I love you."

"I love you too Mom."

I was so thankful that her friend Rachel, was helping her through this, letting her stay with her and holding on to some of her belongings. On the second day after Nana died, Mom was arrested. There was a hearing a week later in which she accepted a plea bargain. About a month after her appalling phone call, Mom was sentenced to twenty years in the Montana Women's Prison on the charge of voluntary manslaughter and would be required to serve eleven of those years.

23 - Nicholas

"Are you sure you have everything?" I was actually looking forward to a little time without Becca around. It wasn't her, necessarily, but there has been so much drama over the past month with her mom and everything I just didn't think I could take any more. "Are you feeling okay?"

"Yeah, I feel good, I think the morning sickness thing is getting better by the day. Let's see, I have clothes for the funeral, pajamas, toothbrush – I'm good babe, I'm only gonna be gone for a couple days."

"I know, well, here we are." She convinced me to drop her off at the airport instead of parking and walking in with her. I parked the car as close as I could get to Delta Airlines and removed her bag from the trunk. As I walked around to her side of the car, I noticed how beautiful she looked. She was only wearing jeans and a dark blue long sleeve t-shirt with little pink flowers on it but she was stunning in her natural state. Her hair was messily tied up and strands fell across her face. She looked at me.

"What?"

"Nothing, you look good." She smiled. "Okay, well you better go or you'll be late."

"Okay, I'll call you when I land in Boston. I love you."

"Love you too." I watched her walk through the automatic doors and melt into the sea of travelers.

As I drove away, I dialed Jason. "Hey man! I'm in town, you wanna get some drinks?"

"Sure, where's Becca?"

"Just dropped her off at the airport, she's off to the east coast for a funeral."

"Sweet! Let's hit the bars! I'll meet you at Ray's."

24 - Rebecca

"Your boarding pass, ma'am. Ma'am?"

"Oh, yes, here. Sorry it's been a long couple of days."

As I boarded the plane back to Denver my mind was filled to the brim with the events of the last two days. I was also thinking about the baby, my sweet baby girl. I hadn't really had a chance to digest this new person in my life and allow it to be real. Here I am becoming a new mom and meanwhile my mother is going to prison for killing her mother. Will I be a good parent? I choked back tears and boarded the plane.

"Excuse me." I had just finished putting my bags in the overhead compartment and was starting to feel just the slightest bit nauseous. There was a man who had to be about my age sitting in the window seat reading a newspaper.

"Yes?"

For a brief moment I couldn't speak. There was something about his eyes and his presence. I have no other way to explain it other than he was able to tug at my heart with just a look. I thought about Nicholas and came to my senses, "I – I'm sorry to even have to ask but," I ducked under the storage bins and sat in the middle seat, "I was wondering if you might switch me seats, I have the middle seat."

"How much is it worth to you?"

"What?" Did I hear him right, is this guy really going to give me crap about switching one seat?

"I'm just kidding! You should have seen the look on your face though!" He smiled and began to get up.

After we were both settled into our seats, I looked over at him, "I'm pregnant." It just spilled out. I can't believe I told a complete stranger, but I feel at ease around him. "I'm pretty much past the morning sickness part but it helps a lot if I can see out the window, so…I really appreciate you switching seats."

"Jack," he put his hand out, "Jack Lauson."

"Rebecca Mitchell, but everyone calls me Becca."

"Well, Becca, anything I can do to prevent you from vomiting on our flight to Denver is my pleasure." He smiled sincerely and I immediately felt better than I had all weekend.

As the plane took off and made its way above the clouds I thought about the funeral, about James and Mom's entire heartbroken family. Without a sound, tears streamed down my cheeks. I've always thought that the *silent cry* is the most desperate of all. I've cried in many ways and many more times than I can count, especially recently; a silent cry speaks the most without saying any words. I wasn't really aware anyone else could see my tears until a tissue appeared in front of me. Damn, how embarrassing. I accepted the tissue and sank in my seat.

"Thanks."

"You okay?" He spoke quietly, which I was grateful for. This was a loaded question. Am I okay? "Yeah, I guess, I just have a lot going on, and to say the least, it's been a tragic few days."

"Well, I'm sorry to hear that. If there's anything I can do." We were both quiet as I soaked up my tears and composed myself. Why not vent to him? In all likelihood, I'll never see him again and he doesn't seem like the judgmental type. "I'm a great listener, you know, just in case you need to listen, I mean, me – someone – to listen." Wow, look who is stumbling over his words now!

"I was in town for a funeral, a family member." I began to tell him everything that had happened over the past two months, what Mom had done and my awkward role as a new mom in all of this, and then I recalled my trip to Boston for Jack without making eye contact. I may never see him again, but I still felt a sense of awkwardness as I conveyed my dirty family secrets.

~

I stepped off the escalator and looked over the sea of people waiting for their bags and noticed James. He looked normal enough in jeans, a paisley sweater and a lightweight green jacket. It's not that I was expecting him to be falling apart but he didn't even appear tired. As I greeted him though, he was pleasant but solemn; trying to make me feel welcome in a place he knew was foreign to me. James is the first-born child so he tends to take the lead in helping his parents, keeping peace between family members and cleaning up messes, like this one. I guess when disaster strikes, someone has to be the one to remain calm and keep everyone else from disintegrating.

He walked me to his Volvo as the snow fell lightly, early for October in Boston. We tried to talk about everything *but* Mom and Nana's death, but it couldn't be avoided. As we drove up to the house, I felt nervous and out of place. I really wasn't sure how her family would receive me but I was hoping for understanding. I'm not exactly sure which family member's house it was but it was beautiful and the biggest house I had ever seen. It was just a few blocks from the coast and a typical New England style home with gray cedar siding and white trim that had a warm presence in the darkness of the evening. The windows glowed with a warm golden light and as we came closer, bags in tow, I heard the unmistakable sound of family.

I walked into the kitchen and was immediately greeted with warm welcomes. *Rebecca! How big you've grown! How was your trip? Here, grab something to eat; you must be starving!* James introduced me to several distant relatives I didn't even know I had, and some that had changed so much over the years, I didn't even recognize. All these people that were my family suddenly surrounded me and I loved it. For a few precious moments I forgot about why I was there and allowed myself to feel part of something bigger than me. After catching up on each other's lives I was taken to my room, exhausted. I called Nicholas to let him know I had landed safely but he didn't pick up. I left him a message then checked the time, I guess it was pretty late but I thought he still might answer.

I glanced over at Jack and was surprised to see him listening intently so I continued. The next day was the one I dreaded. I spent more time getting ready than I have since I was in high school and still it didn't feel right. I still felt slightly nauseous so I asked for some tea as soon as I had the chance. Downstairs, the family gathered again but a much more somber mood had befallen everyone and I remained quiet and pleasant. My other uncle asked how Mom was doing and everyone became quiet. I looked up from my tea a little surprised to see all eyes on me so I just told him that I hadn't talked to her. He mumbled *I just knew she would do something like this one day, she's just not right.* I didn't dare say a word. My own feelings were so mixed up I wasn't sure whether I should defend her or agree with him. This was the only moment I felt completely unwelcome; like Nana's death, was somehow by extension, my fault.

After breakfast, I went for a short walk down to the dock and looked out on the water. I needed to be somewhere else, at least in my mind. I still couldn't believe I was here, in Cape Cod, why would this family even want me here? The cold breeze brightened my cheeks and chilled my bare legs. We all packed into three different cars and drove to the cemetery where there were already people waiting. I stepped out of the car and felt an immediate sense of despair. There must have been fifty people there dressed in darkness, most of which were close family. I never understood before why black was the color of choice to wear for a funeral, why not something celebrating that person's life? But now, I knew that it stood for emptiness and sorrow because that's what the people left behind must endure.

To be honest, I didn't think I would cry. I had never been to a funeral, and to be sure it was a terrible situation, but I had only visited Nana a few times and most of these were when I was a child. I barely knew her. Nana's youngest son, who is a pastor, began to speak with her ashes next to him in a small black box with a gold seal. He spoke poetry of the sea likening its braveness and beauty to her and as he prayed, I allowed my eyes to wander. Her ashes sat on the cold wet ground next to two gravestones belonging to her young sons. I remembered one had died in a car accident on his high school graduation day and one had died at the age of eight from Rheumatic Fever. She would lie in good company. My soul felt heavy and I looked around at my cousins, uncles, aunts, and finally to Granddad. His eyes were glossy and red, his hands shaking and I have never seen a man so lost. Everyone was sobbing like they would simply fall to their knees if the person next to them weren't holding them up. I felt a deeper sadness than I have ever felt and started to weep uncontrollably. Suddenly, it occurred to me that *my* mother had caused all this hurt and pain, all this heartache and misery. I thought of what she told me on the phone and my stomach tightened in pain. If she could only see what she's done.

~

I was crying again and Jack handed me another tissue. "I'm sorry, I shouldn't have told you, I just –." I couldn't say it out loud because I didn't want Jack to think that Nicholas was a bad husband but I still hadn't had a chance to talk to Nicholas and I desperately wanted to hear his voice. I needed comfort and wanted to confide in him. I wanted to tell him all about the last couple of days and for him to tell me it would be okay.

"It's okay, I don't mind." Jack motioned the stewardess over and asked for some water and more peanuts. "It sounds like it's been an emotional rollercoaster for you. I know what you mean about that feeling of having a lot of family around though." I looked over at him.

"Do you have a small family too?" The family that I actually see and keep in touch with is small. I have Megan who I consider family, an older half-sister that I barely talk to, Dad, and grandparents from Dad's side that I get to see once in a while.

"Actually, no." He passed the water and peanuts to me, "Here you go, water cures almost everything! I have a huge family and most of the time I hate it. I guess it's just because I've always had it, you know? I moved away, to Denver and finally got myself some solitude; but when I go home to visit family, I realize every time how much I miss it. Like you said, you feel like you're a part of something bigger."

"I guess you never know what you have until you've lost it."

59

"I guess so."

"So, did you see much of Boston?"

"No, not really, just from the car on the way to the Cape."

"Well, you'll have to check it out some day, lots of history."

Jack went on to talk about all the sights of Boston and curious little towns outside the city. I was relieved that he didn't ask any questions about what I had revealed and that he just let it be. It's just what I needed. Before we knew it, the plane was landing and we were making our way off the plane. He called to me from a few passengers behind, "Becca," I looked back before stepping off the plane, "congratulations."

25 - Megan

"Oh! Thank God, a gas station!" I swerved to take the exit and accidentally cut off the person behind me. "Oops, sorry." I waved a thank you to the car – not that that helps when you're the person being cut off but what are ya gonna do? My butt was numb and my bladder full as I pulled into the Chevron and raced inside.

The drive to Denver isn't too bad and I haven't seen Becca in over a year so I was anxious to get there and probably would have driven to Montana if she were still there! I can't believe she's already six months pregnant. It's hard to believe she's pregnant in general. Why she has to have a child with someone like Nick is beyond me, but I shook that thought from my brain and tried to concentrate on the positives.

With one tank filled and the other emptied I continued on to Denver, only four hours to go. What is it about the highway that brings you to retrace your steps and reminisce? Something about the peaceful monotony lets your mind release the worrisome stuff of life and wander back in time however far you're willing to go. I began to remember Becca and I playing in the fields of grass and buttercups in Montana, riding our bikes down dirt roads and in high school, our long talks about what we would become. We both had big dreams.

Our families moved next to each other on Aster Lane when we were both six years old and since then we've been inseparable. It makes me laugh out loud now thinking back on some of the crazy imaginary lives we would come up with. We would pretend to be sisters and skip around singing in unison. Becca in her brunette braids and me with my golden ponytail traipsed around our family's acreage making up adventures as we went along and not coming home for dinner until we heard the echo of our names.

As the sagebrush and desert landscape passed me by, I recalled one specific memory of a pivotal day in our young lives. We were both about 16 and hanging out in Becca's room talking about the hottest boy in class or something innocent like that. She may have even mentioned Nick at the time but I can't remember. We heard an argument escalate as her parent's voices carried up the stairs. We immediately stopped our conversation to see if we were hearing it right. In all the years I'd known Becca, I had only seen her parents argue once and it was over quickly. Becca seemed just as curious as I was so we tiptoed to the top of the stairs and knelt on the teal carpet.

"You can't be serious!" Becca's mom was screaming in disbelief and crying in between her screams.

"Look, you're the one who chose to screw around."

"I can't believe you're bringing that up again!"

"You bet your ass I'm bringing it up again. So what if I found someone who actually cares about me, it's my decision! You made your choice a long time ago, it's just that it took me awhile to realize that I deserve better."

Becca looked at me in disbelief. Like me, she wasn't sure whether to laugh or cry, was this real? Becca's mom argued with him to the best of her ability but you could tell from the top of the stairs that it was a losing fight.

"I will not tolerate being treated this way anymore! I'm done! Why don't you go back to your little whore!" She said.

We heard the undistinguishable sound of glass crashing to the floor. Becca and I froze in the deafening silence. Footsteps echoed up the hallway and we heard keys scrape the counter.

"No, *I'm* done." A door slammed and we heard a faint cry, Becca jumped to her feet and raced downstairs to her mother.

The rest is a blur, her mother was hysterical one minute and telling Becca everything was fine the next minute. Her mother was never the same after that day. Becca remained close to both her parents though, and that always surprised me because how can you love someone who always chooses themselves over you? But that was Becca, always giving people the benefit of the doubt, always trusting, always loving, almost to the point of her losing herself in the process. I don't think we really understood what happened that day and I'm not sure we ever will. As children crossing the threshold into our version of adulthood, we couldn't possibly grasp the complexities of sustaining a marriage. We became even closer following the argument, and started to see things differently. That roses and rainbows filter of childhood had begun to fade and a more realistic one beginning to take its place.

I crossed the border into Colorado and smiled at the *Welcome to Colorado* sign allowing my mind to wander to some of my most favorite memories. My husband and I love road trips and go whenever we have the opportunity. We've never been out of the country but we haven't even come close to seeing the entire country we live in yet so I figure we have time. Sometimes we just get in the car with a map and a cooler and figure out the details later. I love that about him, I'm the planner and he is the spontaneous one but he is what I sometimes wish I could be. He brings out the spontaneity in me and I suppose I bring out the more practical side in him.

That's what it's all about right? Finding the person who completes you, someone who finishes off where you started and craves your company. It all sounds like the *newly married couple* love and some people say that it can't last, but I disagree. When its right, it lasts but morphs into something different; something that keeps you guessing but comfortable all at the same time.

26 - Rebecca

My swollen feet ached and my back was killing me but I was determined to finish the dishes and clean the house before Megan arrived. Nicholas was supposed to help but he had to work this weekend, or so he said. I rinsed the last glass and looked out the kitchen window.

"Megan!" I screamed like a little girl on Christmas morning. I can't believe she's here. My eyes started to tear from sheer joy. I didn't think I would get this emotional but it's been so long since we've seen each other and, God I missed her. I set the glass in the strainer and ran out the door with my hands dripping wet.

"Ahhh! Megan, I can't believe it's you!" She jumped out of her car and we embraced, both of us crying and laughing.

"Becca! You look gorgeous! Oh, look at your belly, you are so cute!"

"Really, you think so?" I wiped the tears from my face and looked down at my growing belly, "I just feel fat all the time, but thanks." We chatted about her drive and I showed her the house.

Megan set her bag down, "Becca, this is gonna be great. I'm so glad you were able to get the time off while I'm here. We are going baby shopping and we're going to get this room all ready for your little girl!"

"I actually stepped down at work. Nicholas and I thought with the pregnancy and everything I could cut my hours. I requested this time off months ago though!"

I stood there in my future daughter's room not knowing what to say. I hadn't said much to Nicholas about it, but the truth was that I was in panic mode. We hadn't done one single thing to prepare for the baby and it really hadn't felt real until Megan arrived. Nicholas seemed really preoccupied with work since I got back from Boston and keeps telling me that we need to have money if we're going to have a baby. I knew I could count on Megan to save the day. I hugged her again and thanked her for coming.

She made pancakes for dinner and we sat in the living room talking and laughing about old times until I heard Nicholas pull into the driveway. He walked into the house like it took him all the effort in the world and let his keys fall on the kitchen table without saying a word. Both Megan and I looked at him and the moment was starting to feel awkward so I decided to break the ice.

"Hey honey," I pulled myself up off the couch and walked toward him, "Megan's here! How was your day?"

"Oh, hey Megan," he smiled and nodded her way, "how was your trip?"

"Good, thanks. How's work going? Becca tells me you've been busy with a bank project."

He stole a defensive look my way but replied cordially, "Yeah, it's a big project and I've got a lot of guys on it to make sure it goes smoothly. If we do it right, there's a bonus in store for me so it's worth it. I mean, with the baby coming and everything."

"Well, sure. Money is important." Megan looked like she was running out of things to say but doing her best to make everyone feel at ease.

"Babe, there's some pancakes in the oven staying warm if you want some. Megan made 'em."

"Oh, great." He piled up the pancakes and grabbed the syrup bottle, "I'm just gonna take this in the bedroom since I'll probably hit the sack right after I eat." I tried not to make a disgusted face. I could just imagine him pouring half the bottle of syrup on the pancakes until it was just one big soggy pile of carbs and sugar, ugh!

"Oh, okay, yeah – Megan and I will be down here for a while catching up. We're going shopping tomorrow if you want to come." I offered but secretly didn't want him to come.

"No, I definitely won't be joining you." He started laughing a little and Megan and I both joined in.

Megan said, "Yeah, I guess it's kind of a girl thing."

"Good night," Nicholas trudged up the stairs in his work boots holding the plate of pancakes and the bottle of syrup. I couldn't help but think of all the vacuuming I did earlier that day and wondered why I even bothered to clean. Megan must have sensed my disappointment. Best friends are observant that way, noticing the little things that matter to you but might not matter to anyone else. Why can't Nicholas be more observant?

"Becca, hey, don't worry about it, I'll help clean up tomorrow morning before we leave okay?"

I blushed, "Oh, I don't care. It's no big deal."

"Yeah right, if you're anything like me you probably cleaned all day long. Plus you're six months pregnant so it probably took twice as much energy!" We both started laughing hysterically at the thought of me hauling around a vacuum with my bulging stomach and swollen ankles.

Nicholas had left well before Megan and I woke up, which was fine by me. It was nice to not have to worry about the tension building between us. I tried not to think about him. There are so many thoughts running through my mind on a daily basis that I rarely have a chance put them together in a sentence. By the time Nicholas gets home he's tired and doesn't really feel like talking and on the weekends, we are usually doing our own things or spending time with friends so there is little time to ourselves to absorb each other. Without even noticing it, you can become a different person in a matter of weeks and unless you let your significant other in on who you are becoming you can eventually disappear or change completely. I feared that more than anything. I didn't want Nicholas to create his own life outside of *our* life. Not that I didn't want him to have friends, I just didn't want him to become someone else without me, that's all. I guess the same goes for me, I felt myself turning into a different person during this pregnancy and I wanted him to know me and get to know the new me but he just isn't around much.

I shook these plaguing thoughts from my head and waddled down the stairs to find Megan already cooking breakfast.

"You know, you're going to have to let me cook some time so that I can feel like a proper hostess!"

66

Megan smiled as she tossed the scrambled eggs, "Not a chance, I need to feel useful and let's face it, this is the only break you're going to get from your wifely duties so you might as well enjoy it."

"Yeah, you're probably right. Sounds good to me then." I leaned back in the kitchen chair and put my feet up on the chair next to me in an obvious display of relief.

"How's that wonderful husband of yours?" I tried not to sound jealous when I asked the question. They are the type of couple that you watch and just know they were meant for each other. It's depressing to the rest of us normal people. There isn't many out there. There are plenty of good couples, and people that get through the days in a routine sort of way and then there is Megan and Jeff.

"I have only good things to say! He's amazing. His job is going pretty well. He just got a new store and loves the crew he manages but naturally he gets sick of the angry pre-caffeinated customers. I don't know how he does it sometimes."

"I don't know how *you* do it. I thought about working in pediatrics many years ago, remember?"

"I remember." Megan put two pieces of toast in the toaster. "Being a nurse is like anything else, you just get used to it after a while. I guess the human body either fascinates you, disgusts you, or you just never thought much about it."

"Interesting, but true! I guess I fall into the latter category which is probably why I never really went for it, among many other reasons."

"Yes, like boys!" Megan threw a dishtowel at me.

"Damn those boys, they do it every time!" I folded the towel and smiled at her. Time to change the subject. "I can barely contain myself you know, I'm so excited about shopping!"

"Me too, let's talk about what you need."

"I don't have anything Megan. Mom sent me a package of a few things a long time ago but that's all I have so far. Nicholas wanted to wait till we had more money and I'm starting to think we will never have enough money. I mean how much is enough?"

"Well, Becca. That *is* the eternal question isn't it? Don't worry about a thing. I've been saving up and it won't cost Nicholas a precious dime! As I'm sure you know, a little money can go a long way. Besides we're women, thriftiness is one of our specialties."

She served the eggs and toast and we sat in the kitchen enjoying food and each other's company. The last time I sat down at this table and had a meal with someone was when I told Nicholas I was pregnant.

As I lowered myself into her passenger seat, we both started giggling at my awkwardness. I was only six months but everyone kept saying I had to be further along than that because I looked so big. Thanks a lot, I would think to myself.

"Becca, we have two days to shop so there's no reason to push yourself if you're tired okay? You just say the word and we'll stop for something tasty! It will be a good excuse for me too."

Megan and I shopped at thrift stores and Target. I love Target but rarely go there since all I can afford is Wal-Mart. You would think that with a husband as an architect, we would be better off but I guess bills take most of it and who knows what happens to the rest. Someday I'll have the courage to find out. I looked around the room one last time. The walls were painted a light sage green halfway up with a butterfly border separating the wall colors all the way around the room. There was a wooden crib with pink bedding and a changing table/dresser with butterfly knobs. In the dresser was clothes, blankets and many other little toys and necessities. Megan even bought a bright pink and green butterfly rug to match. It was perfect.

"Well, I think that's it!" Megan and I sat on the floor in the middle of the baby's room and I couldn't believe my eyes. Two days ago, the room looked like a storage facility, now it's more beautiful than I imagined! I started to cry.

"Becca? You okay?" She leaned over and put her arm around me.

"Yeah," I wiped the tears from my eyes, "I'm good, I just can't believe you did all this for us."

"Well, for you and the baby – not so much for Nick."

"Well, yeah…anyway it's amazing and I just know she will love it. Abby will love it."

"I must say Becca, it's adorable and if Abby doesn't like it, I'll take it."

"Yeah, me too! I wish my room was this organized."

Megan went quiet a moment and turned to me, "I'm really proud of you Becca. I know you have a lot going on that you don't talk about and you don't have to. Your Mom, Nicholas and having a baby; I know it's a lot and you're really holding it together. I hope Abby inherits your strength."

I didn't know what to say, so I just smiled at her. She said, "If you ever need anything, don't hesitate to call me okay? I don't care what time it is. This is gonna sound a little weird so bear with me."

"Okay."

"I know sometimes you hesitate to tell me things for whatever reason, and that's okay. I'm on your side Becca and I could never think badly of you for a decision you made that you think is right for you. I might not agree, but it doesn't mean I don't love you. You're like a sister to me. Don't forget it okay?"

"Okay." I hugged her and held on for dear life. I'm sure she could feel my desperation. She would be leaving at dawn tomorrow and with her, would go my safety net. With Megan around I was more confident, more excited about the future and more certain that I deserved better from Nicholas. She reassured me somehow that my expectations weren't too high. It will be too long before I see her again.

27 - Nicholas

"Alright Carl, good work today man. Before you know it, we'll have this thing finished! See you tomorrow seven, sharp." I walked out the door and hopped into my truck with a sigh of relief.

Finally, my day was over. This project was taking much longer than I had calculated and costing more too, which is just taking money away from my paycheck in the end. It's brilliant though. It's a new design, much more modern than the other branches in the Denver area. Since the bank is going next to the new *up and coming* neighborhood, Rocky Mountain Estates, it had to be something unique, and thanks to me, it is. As I pulled onto the highway toward home, where my *very* pregnant wife was waiting, my phone rang. I glanced down to the cup holder where the phone was sitting and noticed the caller, Jenna. I didn't dare answer it. I didn't want her to think that we had anything going on just because we made out one lousy night.

Jenna was beautiful though, but in a more dolled up sort of way, whereas Becca has this natural beauty and plainness about her. Jenna is curvy and blonde with an amazing sense of humor and much more outgoing. I'm not saying that's better or worse – just different. It happened the night Becca took off to the east coast for a funeral. I went out with Jason to Ray's and a bunch of friends ended up there, drinkin' and playin' pool. I haven't had that much fun in a long time. Becca and I used to go out like that but we haven't done it since school, then my new job and now, with the baby. I'm sure I'm doomed to a life of boredom so I figure I might as well get it where I can.

"Hey, how are my girls!" I throw my keys on the table and kiss Becca and allow a brief flash of Jenna to enter my mind. I kiss her growing belly. Time is flying by and her due date is just around the corner. I know this because she reminds me daily as if I anticipated her being pregnant forever.

"I can't believe how big you are." The house smells so good. I can already taste the pot roast and mashed potatoes. As I take my boots off and look up at Becca staring at me with tears welling up in her eyes.

"What?"

"I've been cleaning and cooking half the day and all you can say is 'I can't believe how big you are?' Seriously?"

You've got to be kidding me. She's been like this for the last couple months, teetering on the cusp of emotional instability. Everything I say and do is wrong and she twists it into something I couldn't have even predicted.

"Honey, I didn't mean it that way and you know it. You're pregnant for God's sake! Of course, you're big. That's good right? Healthy baby?" I walked closer to her. I am so tired. I really don't feel like stroking her ego right now. Can't she just understand I didn't mean it that way and get over it? Must I constantly reassure her? "You're beautiful, okay?"

I wiped a tear from her eye and she starts to smile. All I could think was *thank God*. I didn't have the energy to go through an entire exhausting conversation. She began transferring the food from the oven to the table.

"How was work?" she asked.

"Oh, fine. We're getting closer to being finished, just a little longer."

"Good, I can't wait to see it when it's done!"

I walked upstairs to squeeze in a shower before dinner. I'd make it quick.

"Nicholas, where are you going?"

"Shower." I kept walking.

"Are you kidding? I'm setting the table. Dinner is ready right now."

"Becca, I'll just be a couple minutes."

"Can't you shower after? Its gonna get cold and it won't taste as good. I've been cooking all day!"

I threw my hat toward the bedroom, frustrated and stomped down the stairs. I can't wait till she has this damn baby; maybe things will get back to normal. "Fine, I'll eat right now." I have to admit I was being a little dramatic, exaggerating each movement and slamming dishes and silverware where I could. It wasn't necessary, but I just wasn't in the mood for this right now.

"So, now you're going to be angry through the whole meal?" She dished out my mashed potatoes and vegetables. Despite my growing anger, I was hungry and the food looked delicious. "Nicholas, I just wanted you to be able to enjoy the meal that's all. You can shower after, right?"

I remained silent, just trying to enjoy the meal in peace and quiet.

"What's wrong now?" Was she really going to do this tonight? She never used to talk to me like this.

"I just can't wait till you have this baby and for things to go back to the way they used to be!"

"What is that supposed to mean?"

"You know what, you're just different. I don't know. Never mind, okay, let's just enjoy dinner." I was trying to avoid fighting. Not only did I not have the energy, but I always end up being the bad guy – no matter what the circumstances are. It's never her fault.

She was quiet for a moment and then I was surprised at the calmness in her voice. The question came out in a sincere, inquisitive tone almost as if her being different might be a good thing. "What do you mean different? Like how?"

I shoveled a heaping forkful of pot roast and potatoes in my mouth, looked over at her and shrugged. She started to eat too, almost like she had let down her guard and I thought Y*es! No fight, it's amazing!*

Then I opened my big mouth, "It's just since Megan left, I guess. I don't know something is different."

"Hmm, well it doesn't sound like you think it's a good thing."

"I don't! You're rude and self-centered and you never think about me anymore. Megan is just like that too and I think she's a bad influence on you. Thank God she lives in Arizona or I'd have to deal with it all the time."

The silence should have been my first clue, but I was so satisfied with myself and how I had finally been able to tell her what I had been feeling these last few months, that I didn't notice.

"Megan is my best friend and might as well be my sister! She has always been there for me, so don't you dare go there! I don't tear apart your friends!" She stood abruptly and began cleaning. She always does this when she's agitated.

"I wasn't tearing her apart, I was simply telling you that you're being a bitch and you get it from her."

"What? Did you just call me a *bitch*?" She picked up a wooden serving spoon, the closest thing to her and chucked it at me. "Well, you're an asshole! If anything, I'm a stronger person because of Megan and you don't like that because then you don't get every little thing you want."

"All I wanna do is come home and have a nice quiet dinner with my wife and take a god damn shower whenever I damn well please!" I threw the serving spoon back at her.

"You know what Nicholas, the world doesn't revolve around *you* all the time!"

"Well, it should!" I was getting in over my head but she was pushing me. If she didn't push me, I wouldn't have to do this. She stopped dead in her tracks; I seemed to have thrown her off guard.

"What? The world should revolve around you? Are you kidding me? We are about to have a *baby* Nicholas! The world revolves around the baby, not you! If anyone's self-centered it's you!"

"Rebecca, you're my wife and you'll do what I say. If you don't like it, then you can just leave. I'd love to see you walk out that door and make it on your own. You don't have anything, no skills, no money, nothing!" Becca and I were both screaming so loud that our voices were going hoarse. She was crying and her face was wet and beet red but I was so angry, I didn't care. I wanted to walk out the door myself. Then I thought, why not?

"Fuck you!" She was sobbing uncontrollably now. I don't need this shit. I slipped into my shoes and went to the closet to grab my coat.

"Ahhh!" Becca's scream echoed in a twisted agonizing tone. I whipped around about to tell her off and she was leaning on the couch and crouched over with her head down.

"Becca?" I dropped my coat and ran toward her. She was on her knees now clinging to the arm of the couch. I reached out and grabbed her arm trying to comfort her in some way.

"Don't touch me!" she screamed and then wobbled, screaming again in pain. Evidently that changed her mind because she grabbed me by the shirt and looked me straight in the eye.

"Nick, there's something wrong. It hurts!" Becca grabbed her belly with her free hand and screamed again with her teeth clenched.

I began to panic just a little, "What do we do? We should go to the hospital!"

Becca started to cry again. "I think my water just broke." She whispered a barely audible *I'm scared.*

I thought, *me too.*

28 - Eveline

"Let's go ladies, rise and shine!" The guards make the rounds, releasing me from all the terror the night brings. I've been here for nine months and twenty days now, not that I'm counting, and they've relocated me four times. I cried every day for the first few months but they kept putting me in the wing with the insane people so I had to find a way to overcome my despair or at least mask it, which is all I was able to do. I still cry once in a while, but I do it silently and only when no one is around. The night is the worst for me since I am left to my own thoughts and memories of what once was and what could have been. I feel it will haunt me forever, even when I get out of this hellhole.

I hadn't heard from Rebecca in a couple of months, until today. I always go to mail call even though most days are a letdown. It keeps my hopes up though, and gives me something to look forward to as part of my daily routine. Today when they called me, *Kerner! Mail!* I nearly jumped out of my skin reaching for that beautiful white envelope. I held it close to me as I briskly walked down the hallway, past the door to the visiting room, past the corridors of iron bars and finally to my cell. Usually there are two other women in the room but today was Tuesday, lucky for me, because on Tuesdays Jamie has Bible study and Terry has an English class she goes to. She came here speaking nothing but Spanish so she's trying to work on her English. I climbed onto my bunk, took one last look around and opened the envelope.

After reading the letter meticulously three times, I sat back against the cold cement wall and smiled for the first time in months. A beautiful baby girl named Abigail Rae Mitchell. I'm officially a grandmother! I hid the letter under my mattress so I could read it again later. Rebecca sounded pretty good, but she mostly talked about Abigail, every little detail of her, and what it was like to be a mom. I allowed my mind to wander back to the first time I looked at Rebecca. She was the most precious thing I had ever seen and for the first time in my adult life, I knew what it felt like to truly love someone unconditionally. There were many days I questioned my love for my husband or my parents but Rebecca was different. I knew right then and there that I would do anything for her.

Suddenly, I felt a deep sense of disappointment wash over me. I suppose life takes over sometimes and even though my love for her never changed, I'm sure I have let her down many times over. I mean, look at me! I'm in prison for Christ's sake! I should be happy, ecstatic really, that I'm a grandmother and that Rebecca and Abigail are both healthy, but then I open my eyes and remember where I am and what I'm doing here. I see bars in front of me and the rusted sink and toilet in the corner and become angry. I was a teacher! A damn *good* teacher at that. I have a PhD and yet here I am with the scum of the earth.

I hear a barrage of footsteps and realize that all the morning classes must be over. I wipe my eyes and climb down from my bunk just as Terry comes around the corner.

"Hola Eveline!" she is usually in a good mood after English class so I take advantage of that when I can. She was sentenced to eight years for stabbing her husband after he raped her. There is so much injustice in this world. It comes in all forms.

"Hola Terry, how was English?" I asked as I stuffed the envelope under my mattress.

"Okay, I still think I would learn a lot more from you. I tell you, talk to Mr. Grant about teaching. I mean, with you a teacher he be happy to have you!"

"Yeah, I've been thinking about it, I just might do that." I was going crazy with all the free time. I never really noticed it before I went to prison, but if I don't stay busy, I go stir-crazy. I'm just now getting to the point where the guards are seeing me as more of a 'stable' person and I've been working really hard to stay on everyone's good side. This is not an easy task because what the inmates want and what the guards want are two very different things.

In the first month I was here, I remember Terry and Jamie being part of a gang of women that cheered on my initiation. Every inmate has to endure some sort of torture, a test of strength to see which clique they belonged to. For me, they had approached me during yard call. Women of all shapes and sizes surrounded me shouting taunts and poking at me with their fingers and throwing dirty tampons at me. I was so frightened and unsure of what the appropriate reaction should be I kept quiet at first, ducking when I could. I had never been around people like this before and I struggled to understand everything about them. I still felt I was distinctly different from them in many ways.

They began pushing me around the circle, back and forth then punching and kicking me as I fell to the frozen ground. When minutes passed by and no one came to my rescue, no guard, no inmate, nothing, I realized that I could die here on this cold ground alone if I didn't fight back. I allowed all the anger I had ever felt toward anyone in my life to surface. My memories of being bullied at home and on the playground flooded my mind and I rose to my feet in a quick maneuver surprising not only myself but all the inmates, half of who had given up on seeing a good fight. I struck back with all the strength I had – which wasn't much compared to some of these women. I struck Jamie in the face and as soon as I did everyone stopped beating me and started clapping.

I hadn't the faintest idea as to what just happened, but I knew I was alive, and for this I was thankful. As soon as everyone left the yard and I stood alone, I fell to the ground covered my head and cried until I felt a guard's presence. I quickly wiped my eyes like nothing had happened and walked past him back to my cell. The guards participated in these initiations just as much as the inmates by allowing it to happen. Upon this realization I knew there was not one person I could depend on, no one I could trust but myself, and sometimes this was even up for debate. Jamie, Terry and I now had an understanding, not a friendship. There were no friendships here. This place was lifeless and hollow like so many of its residents.

When I'm sitting here in this cell staring through the bars to a grey world beyond, I can feel the depression settle into my soul, attempting to make a permanent home. Thank God I have Rebecca, she is what keeps me going every day. Just the thought of being able to see her again without a barrier between us prevents me from following through with some of the destructive thoughts I entertain. When it seems like there is no point in living, I remember her, and now I will think of Abigail too.

29 - Rebecca

"Can you believe she's six months old today?" I asked Nicholas as he stared at the television.

He sighed and lifted himself out of the chair, probably being coaxed more by the smell of food than anything. I hadn't really been cooking meals for the past six months and this past week I've just begun to feel a little better and more motivated to take care of the house and everything. Mostly I've been immersing myself in Abigail; bottles, diapers, laundry and my most favorite thing – play time! I call her Abby because it suits her; she's perfectly adorable. I look over at her little round face and bright eyes and just the very presence of her fills me with joy. I never thought I could love someone this much. Her hair was blonde when she was born but it is starting to look much more like mine, a deep brown. Her eyes are her most stunning feature, a bright mixture of gray, green and brown crystallized together with long eyelashes curling around them. Her personality is starting to shine through as she grows. Her smile and her grumpy little pout when I just don't understand what she wants. I love it all.

Nicholas bent down over her and tickled her, "You're six months old today Abby! Yes, you are!" He turned to me, "Is dinner almost ready? I'm starving and it smells delicious!"

"Yep, five more minutes."

"It's been a while since you've made a meal like this."

"I know, I just haven't felt like myself lately –"

"It's nice." He moved in closer to me and pulled me toward him by the small of my back, kissing my neck. I still thought about the night I went into labor and the argument we had. I'm positive one of us would have left if things had been different that night, but after Abby was born, I just felt like we owed it to her to give it a shot. It was as if she was trying to bring us together. I remember lying in the hospital with Abby in my arms and Nicholas's arms around us – a beautiful happy family. At that moment with Abby in my arms and my husband cradling us, I wondered if our happiness was real or if it was just an illusion of my own making. Sometimes, when you want something bad enough, you make believe it's real at any cost without even realizing it. I did it once before when I met Nicholas. He was my knight in shining armor on a white horse with a rose in his hand. What girl wouldn't want that fairytale?

Nicholas's voice echoed in my mind as I stirred the pasta sauce and thought about Megan encouraging me to use my talents, then Nicholas's taunt. *I'd love to see you walk out that door and make it on your own. You don't have anything, no skills, no money, nothing!* I have skills, you just don't know it.

"Nicholas?" I turned the burners on the stove off and began bringing delicious steaming dishes to the table.

"Yeah?" He was standing with one foot on the kitchen linoleum and one on the carpet staring at the TV. He kept his eyes on the TV but nodded his head in my direction. He wanted to appear as if he was listening while still paying attention to what was more important at the time – probably some golf show.

"Hey, I was thinking…hi sweetie," I cooed to Abby as I put her bib on, "you ready for some yum yums? What do you think about me catering? Cooking, you know?"

I finished putting all the condiments on the table and pulled back the napkins to reveal hot golden-brown biscuits.

"Dinner's ready!" I sat down and Nicholas turned and sat down to the right of me so I could feed Abby. He was giddy with hunger.

"Bec, this looks good! Mmmm."

"So, what do you think?" He took in a mouthful and looked adoringly at Abby.

"About what babe."

"About me catering."

"Do you mean you'd work for someone else or start your own business?"

Glad to see he was willing to entertain the idea, I continued the conversation, "I don't know, maybe a little bit of both, I'm not really sure. I just wanted to talk about it. You like my cooking, right?"

"Yes! I love your cooking, but it's different cooking for hundreds of people Becca. You just had Abby and there's still a lot to do around the house. Starting your own business is a lot of hard work. Are you sure you're ready for that? We can't afford full time day care for Abby right now." I had already quit my job at Whole Foods just before I had Abby and I was feeling useless with all this free time. Well, *free* is relative with a newborn but it was a difficult adjustment for me.

"I know, I was just thinking about starting small, just doing a few things here and there you know? Besides," his insult to my work ethic just registered, "who put you're a-s-s through school working three jobs, don't tell me about hard work. Have you ever been in labor? You don't even know what hard work is!" I was pushing my luck but I was so insulted by his comment I couldn't help but get defensive. Oddly enough, he didn't seem to mind my feistiness.

"Well," he smiled and leaned back in his chair as if to say *well, look who's got gumption. Okay, you think you can do it? Go ahead.* "Give it a shot then, if that's what you want. As long as it doesn't take away from us, we don't have a lot of extra money to put toward it but if you can work with what we've got then go for it."

"Okay, great!" I was glowing with excitement and pride that he thought I would be good at it. I looked over at Abby and made a funny face causing an uproar of giggles and bubbles to erupt from her lips. I placed my hand over his and met his eyes and thought, *aren't we lucky.*

It's been months since we've been intimate in any way and about a week after our conversation, I realized I missed it. I was finally to the point where I could look in the mirror at my nakedness and say, *not bad Becca.* I know Nicholas has been going crazy so that night I decided to surprise him. I put Abby to bed early and waited for Nicholas to get home from work.

As we were making love, I was strangely distracted with various things, did I leave the nightlight on for Abby, could I be a caterer, and then it occurred to me that Nicholas hadn't taken a shower in…let's see…five days…could it be? It's an odd time for thoughts like that but I couldn't help it, it was like an epiphany and those don't come often. It's not that I wasn't enjoying myself but something was different between us. Our rhythm had changed and I couldn't catch on. I counted backward and marked each day by a memory. Wednesday I went to get groceries, Thursday I met with Jill about watching Abby, Friday and Saturday were the lonely do-nothing days and yesterday I took Abby to the park and Nicholas came home around seven. Nicholas had only been home for dinner two of those days and as I scrolled through them, I couldn't remember him taking a shower. Lately, he has been going on short trips for work, meeting with the big wigs of the bank and other contracting firms that have been working on this bank project. He's come home every night of course but never taken a shower. I guess I should be disgusted except for the fact that he smells as clean as can be, which leads me to believe one thing. He must be showering somewhere else. Just the fact that I have to think about these things is ridiculous!

I should be able to trust my husband without question, if something doesn't make sense, I should be able to ask and he should be able to explain without getting defensive. I tried to push the thought from my mind but it was still there dangling in the background as a '*what if*'. I didn't want him to know anything was wrong, so I just faked an orgasm. He didn't seem to notice the difference anyway or if he did, he didn't care. I've had to do it before and it's not like it's difficult, so that seemed to satisfy him.

We cleaned up and he went into the kitchen for a snack. I peeked into Abby's room and saw her beautiful little face, fast asleep with the butterfly nightlight glowing in the corner. Every time I look at her, I can't help but smile. I walked downstairs and sat down at the kitchen table with a glass of water. Why shouldn't I ask, maybe he'll understand. I mean it's a valid question that any sane person would ask. I would expect him to ask me if he noticed I hadn't showered in five days.

"How ya doin'?"

"Good." He looked over at me while he poured his coffee. "You?"

"Good, it's good to have you home for a while, especially this time of night. I – I noticed you haven't showered here in a while…" I can't believe I'm asking this question. Deep breath. "Are you . . . showering somewhere else? You know – Jason's or something?" I tried to sound casual but I'm sure it came out stuttering and nervous sounding. We've had conversations like this before while he was going to school. I would feel like something wasn't right and he would swear up and down that he would never want anyone but me and then it would just result in me feeling ridiculous for even *thinking* he could be seeing someone else. It was *my* fault.

He took a slow, calculated sip of his coffee and gently set the cup on the counter. The calmness was uncanny and I braced myself.

"I'm *not* cheating on you, if that is what you are asking, I don't know how many times I have to tell you that Becca." Every word was concise and deliberate backing me into a corner.

"I didn't say that, I was talking to Jason the other day while we were waiting for you and I was just –," he interrupted me, slamming his hand down on the counter so hard that my body shook and his coffee rippled.

"When I give you an answer, that's it, you accept it. You don't keep asking me questions, or go around asking people about me. That is completely unacceptable!" He took a step toward me and met my eyes, "*You* listen to *me* and that's the end of it. I don't want to hear any more about it."

He slowly picked up his coffee and walked past me into the living room. I was in shock. Did he just tell me 'how it was going to be'? What are we, in the 1950s? Despite my frustration and feeling of being belittled, a grin crept across my face and I had to put my hand over my mouth to hide it. I couldn't help but think of that line from the Disney movie Oliver and Company and how badly I wanted to say it straight to Nicholas's face. *Isn't it dangerous to use one's entire vocabulary in a single sentence?* He would shit a brick.

30 - Rebecca

It's funny how a person can be good in one role and a whole other person in a different role. I realize this as I sit across from my husband at Pioneer Pizza and Abby is pulling a napkin along with all of the silverware off the table. He is so patient and kind and aware of her now, so in tune with her needs, at least for this moment. How is it that he can be this patient man as a father in fleeting moments such as this, and as a husband someone that is neglectful and selfish? It made me question myself. Am I someone else too? Am I that different when I am a wife, a mother, or a friend? I have never thought of myself as a person in just one individual role; always a wife, mother, daughter, coworker and friend rolled into one, juggling them simultaneously. Nicholas has a chance to separate them or sometimes avoid them altogether. He gets to wake up in the morning before Abby gets up and head off to work in his own vehicle, probably listening to his favorite CD on his way in. He comes home, takes a shower and sits on the couch because "he works so hard, he deserves a break" still having no part in being a father to Abby. If it's a good day he might play with Abby for a bit before I give her a bath and put her to bed, leaving me to hold onto all of my thoughts and happenings of the day until she is asleep. That's when I anticipate a connection, but most of the time there is nothing there, just space. Then there are times when we do connect and he finally morphs – or is forced into – the role of a husband again for a few moments before he drifts off in front of the television.

Sometimes I'm so angry. I guess jealous is more the word I'm looking for. It's just not fair that I have to run a household, be a mother and a wife, work and keep it all together without a break. I am forced to give up things I would rather do for what I *have* to do and it seems that he never has to make that sacrifice. On top of that, he doesn't seem to have any empathy for the fact that I *do* have to make that sacrifice. All he sees is himself, what he wants and what he thinks he deserves. What about me? What about us?

It' as if I am not really there but just a shadow looking on from a corner. After a half-ass conversation that is mostly about him, I check on Abby to get away. I close the door only halfway so that some light spills into her room and she doesn't feel alone. There is nothing worse than loneliness. There's no quick fix and it's deep inside you where no one else can see it. It's unfortunate, because it's one of the few feelings I wish could be obvious to others. Anger and jealousy are feelings most people wish they could conceal. If loneliness were like anger, people would look at you, know your sense of emptiness and maybe even want to make it better. But unfortunately, it's hidden deep inside for no one to discover until it's too late or until you have the courage to reveal it all on your own. Alone. How ironic.

31 - Nicholas

"Becca, tonight's the party remember? How could you forget, I've been looking forward to this day for months!" The bank project is finally finished and everyone at work including some of our other friends, are meeting for drinks and dinner at a steakhouse in town. Jill, a friend of Becca's, who I don't really care for, is here to watch Abby but Becca isn't even ready yet. Evidently, she forgot.

"Honey, I didn't really forget, I just spaced it today that's all – it's been a really hectic week for me! I had doctor's appointments for Abby and me, errands to run and that interview with Good Eats catering company." I gave her a look and then looked at my watch.

"Bec, we're gonna be late!"

"Two minutes, I promise." She ran up the stairs and into the bedroom while I waited downstairs. I can't believe I'm going to be late to my own celebration. Damn Becca! It's always about her. I walked over to Jill and plucked Abby from her arms.

"Hey sweetie! Are you gonna miss Daddy? You be a good girl okay?" I placed Abby on the floor in front of her toys and walked anxiously to the bottom of the stairs. Truthfully, I was really looking forward to a night away from the house and away from the responsibilities of Abby. I loved her more than I've loved anyone in the world – even more than I love Rebecca. Sometimes, though, all I want to do is whatever the hell I want and it's almost impossible with a baby. We're awake off and on throughout the night and always worried about scheduling our lives around Abby. I couldn't wait to just enjoy a night of pats on the back. I worked really hard to finish this project, I deserved a little appreciation damnit.

"Becca! Really?" I saw a red flash go from the bedroom to the bathroom then she came barreling down the stairs in her bare feet, shoes dangling from her fingers and a red dress that would make any man drool.

"Wow."

"You like it?" She didn't wait for my reaction. She grabbed her coat and gave a list of instructions to Jill that I thought would never end while I stared at her in disbelief. The dress was one that I had only seen her wear once before; a cocktail dress that had a plunging but elegant neckline, frilly shoulders, and stopped at her knees. I thought about Jenna and how she would probably be wearing a much shorter and tighter skirt.

"Okay," I said as I took Becca's arm and slid her out the door. She was almost in tears leaving Abby. "Bye Jill! Thanks!"

"Maybe I shouldn't go," she said as she stood by the passenger door.

"Becca, get in."

We made it to the party just as everyone else was ordering their drinks. There were so many people there I had to search through the crowd to find someone I knew. Finally, I spotted Jason and some guys from work.

"Jason! Hey man, what's up?"

"Here's the man of the hour! Congratulations bro. A beautiful building, really."

Frank, Jim and Allan chimed in with more congratulations and handshakes. Before I knew it, everyone was buying me drinks.

"Oh, you guys remember Becca."

"Well, hello Becca! How are you? How's the baby?"

"Good, she's great, thanks. A big night huh?"

"Yep, how does it feel to be married to a brilliant architect?"

She looked over at me but wasn't given a chance to answer since more people showed up and began crowding around us laughing and telling stories about the project. I spotted Jenna sitting at the bar with a margarita and didn't turn away as quickly as I should have. When I turned my attention back to the crowd, I caught Becca's eye.

It wasn't until hours later when most of our friends had left, that I had a chance to track Becca down again. She was sitting at a table in the bar section of the restaurant with Amanda, a friend of ours since we moved to Denver. Amanda is married to a guy that

I've met a few times, but Becca and I have only had dinner with them once or twice and only see Amanda at big events like this, so they probably had some catching up to do.

"Ladies."

"Nicholas," said Amanda, surprised. "Look who finally had time to come over and say hi."

"Well, I'm popular tonight I guess, what can I say?" I half joked and grabbed a stool.

"Hey Bec, how ya doin'?"

"Fine. I called Jill, Abby's asleep and she said she had a good night. In case you were wondering."

"Right, well, I hope she's asleep it's two a.m. for God's sake," I laughed a little too hard as I was still reeling from all the drinks and only partially regretted it.

"We should probably get going Amanda. My husband will be falling asleep shortly and I'm anxious to get home."

"Well, Becca, it was so good to see you! You call me if you need to talk or, just anything okay?" They hugged each other and I felt Becca tug at my sleeve.

"What were you two talking about? How bad a husband I am?"

"What? Hardly, you're drunk. How about we save the pleasant conversation for when you're sober okay?"

Becca was telling Jason congratulations and goodbye as well as giving him reasons for our early departure so with any luck, she didn't over hear Jenna whispering in my ear, "Let me know when your wife goes out of town again."

32 - Megan

Why is it that Becca can't see how destructive Nicholas is to her sense of self and that she deserves so much better? It's a textbook abusive relationship. The man is charming (my most unfavorite quality in a person because of what it usually means) and attentive for the first six months or a year then things start to change. It could be slow change or it could be in a sudden burst of behavior that is 'out of character'. It could be months or years of this yo-yo like relationship where things are going *so well* then *so horrible*, then back again. This chaotic symphony becomes the language of the relationship and often not realized that it's not okay until one of them sees how good someone else has it or sees another relationship that mirrors their own. Then you say to yourself, is that me? Is that my life? No, my relationship isn't *that* bad. By the time you realize your being treated like a doormat, your self-esteem is so low you don't think you deserve anything better. This is life. Life has ups and downs, right? You justify the hell out of it to make yourself feel better.

I should know, because I lived it for a year and a half. I was only in high school but that's when girls are primed to be taken advantage of because most don't know any better. I never married the guy, thank God, and its nothing like what Becca has had to deal with, but the concept is the same. It's even more difficult to watch someone you love have to go through it. I think this is why I decided I never wanted children – well, one of the reasons. I'm not saying it doesn't cross my mind once in a while, but I don't want to worry all the time and to watch the bad things that will inevitably happen. I don't want to watch helplessly while my daughter dates a bastard she thinks is God's gift to women, or to watch my son get involved with friends who don't have his best interests at heart, friends who are not really friends. I know all that is a part of life, a part of learning about oneself, but for me, I think it would just be too painful to watch as a parent. It's a little easier, I would imagine, as a friend or even a sibling, so I'll just stick to that. There is another reason that I don't want children and I don't tell many people, especially those that have kids because it ends up coming out as an insult somehow, instead of just my own personal feelings. I love being married, I love spending time with Jeff and I don't want anything to take away from that. We just never get tired of each other. Don't get me wrong, we go out separately with our friends sometimes, we do our own things too, but it never gets old to be us.

One of my patients at Scottsdale Healthcare is a 5-year-old girl who has recurring tumors on her left kidney and has been in and out of the hospital since she was three. Today she asked me a question that threw me for a loop as I was getting her last set of vitals before leaving for the day.

"Megan?" She ignored my actions as I moved around her checking monitors and tubes as if she wasn't attached to them. She was a pro at this, and unlike her parents, rarely thought about her condition. Instead, she would talk about butterflies, dancing, and how she wanted to be a nurse someday too.

"Yeah?" I was focused on her vitals, which were stable but could be a lot better.

"Why do grownups fight so much?"

I stopped in the middle of assessing her blood pressure and looked into her bright brown eyes. How do I answer that? There are so many reasons and as I thought of the list of excuses, none of them seemed valid. I could only assume she was referring to her parents. I had overheard them fighting in her room while they thought she was asleep, arguing in the hall about her care and about personal things between them. It's not my place as a nurse to get involved. My main concern is to put my patient first, so she was my priority.

As I stuttered and looked up at the ceiling and out the window trying to find an answer I thought about Becca, Nick and now they had Abby. God, they could fight. I thought of Becca's shaky voice on the phone after many of these moments, angry at something he had done or said or something he hadn't done or said. In the next breath, as I tried to convince her she deserved better than that, and so did Abby, she would find a way to justify his actions. It wasn't his fault, he is stressed out with work, she was expecting too much. It was always something.

I looked at my little patient and brushed the hair out of her face, "People fight because they are afraid, but that doesn't mean it's okay." I finished taking her blood pressure and straightened out her bedding. As I turned to leave, I said, "You know, not *all* grownups fight that much." I gave her a wink and closed the door. How do you answer those complicated questions in a few sentences that took you several years to figure out yourself?

33 - Rebecca

I defend him and fear him in the same sentence. I'm so scared and so mad at myself for allowing myself to get into this situation.

"It's not like I hate him, but I know where it's going and that he'll never change." I spoke to myself in the car trying to get up the courage to do what I was about to do. Abby was asleep in her car seat with her head flopped to the side and a red juice stain on her mouth. I tried to fall apart quietly so that I didn't wake her.

It was like being raped over the phone. I couldn't scream for help. I just had to lie there and take it. Nicholas was supposed to be at work but when I went to bring him a surprise lunch, I found out he wasn't there. He wouldn't tell me where he was, once I got him on the phone and he managed to make it my fault that I had expected him to be there. The last month had just been one shitty thing after another. He would say that his paycheck was less than it was and take the money and spend it, God knows where. I discovered his paycheck tucked between the driver's seat and the console as I was cleaning the truck. Then there was Jenna whispering in his ear the night we went to his work party. I only caught bits and pieces but it was enough to make me suspicious.

Every time I questioned him, he was a ticking bomb starting out quiet and innocent. *How could you think that? I would never lie to you.* Then he would explode like a volcano with a look on his face that makes my knees buckle in fear just thinking about it and words that would cut deeper than any physical pain could. I couldn't take it anymore. I just kept looking at Abby, so beautiful and innocent and happy and then I would look in the mirror and see a sad, scared, empty woman. After this last conversation, I looked at my sleeping baby and decided right then and there that I didn't want Abby to grow up with this relationship as her model of how relationships should be - and think I'm okay with it. Nicholas would never go to counseling in a million years because he didn't think anything was wrong with him, it was *me* who just had to know my place then everything would be fine.

I pulled into the lawyer's office that I had literally picked out of the phone book and carried Abby in with me. Today, it would end. Things were going to change.

34 - Jack

I thanked the guy at the register for my turkey sandwich and headed out the door. Most of the time I condemned progress. Why does there have to be a Subway at every shopping center or business center in town? Why do a Lowe's and a Home Depot have to go in where each new development goes up? But today, I was thankful. I was starving and this was the only place where you could get something healthy to eat close to my work. I opened the door to my car and threw my sandwich on the passenger seat. I looked up just before getting into my car and did a double take. She was no more than thirty feet away across the parking lot walking toward me but looking at the office building ahead. Could it be her? I took off my sunglasses to make sure I wasn't dreaming. I had thought of her every day since the plane ride and she was even more beautiful than I remembered. She was carrying a baby wrapped in a pink blanket and juggling her purse on the other shoulder.

It occurred to me that I should say something to get her attention before she was gone forever. Just as I opened my mouth to call out her name, I saw her enter the Law Offices of Bernard & Henrietta Fisk. I couldn't do it. I didn't know why she was going into a law office but I could guess and if I was right, I certainly didn't want to get in the middle of anything. She literally had her hands full. Her face looked red and tired as if she had been crying so much that she had run out of tears. I just stared after her and ached to help her in some way. All I wanted to do was hold her and that little baby and tell them everything would be okay. Some things just aren't meant to be, I guess.

35 - Nicholas

"Who the hell do you think you are?" A divorce? Are you kidding me? Where does she get off making decisions like that? I tried to compose myself but I felt everything that I had worked so hard for slipping through my fingers. I had everything I wanted; a beautiful wife, a child, and a great job which was getting better every year. Why would she take it all away from me?

"Look, Bec, I know things have been rough lately but it'll get better – I'll get better." She bit her lip as she slid the paperwork toward me. "You won't change your mind, will you? What about Abby?" I started to choke on my words when I spoke of my little girl. She was all that was good in this world.

"I would never take her away from you Nicholas, we have to put together a parenting plan that would help us figure out how we can split up our time with Abby fairly. We'll be staying at Amanda's until I can get my own place." It was then that a selfish thought crossed my mind. I would have more free time after this was all over. I could come and go as I pleased, I could spend time with Abby whenever I wanted and I wouldn't have to answer to anyone. It was starting to sound appealing, as was Jenna's offer – no strings attached.

"Look, Becca, let's make this as painless as possible okay? I'll sign whatever you want." I grabbed the paperwork still in disbelief that any of this was happening. "You know, it could have worked if you would just give it a chance." I slid it back across the table to her.

Her eyes swelled with tears but none fell. She grabbed her keys and folded the paperwork into an envelope.

"You're out of chances."

36 - Rebecca

Adrenaline filled my body; I had to get out before I fell apart in front of him. Megan once described it to me as *fight or flight*, epinephrine and norepinephrine, hormones being released from my adrenal glands into my bloodstream. I was picturing this as I walked out the door with the divorce paperwork in hand. Each and every blood vessel was bursting. *Fight or flight.* One day I hoped that I would be able to channel that energy and anger into saying something profound when I really wanted to or doing something brave, right there in the moment. For now, though, when I felt the adrenaline rush through my body, I felt scared and unsure and I knew if I didn't get out, I would break down and either scream at him or take him back. Neither option is probably a good idea right now.

I called Megan to get reassurance that I was doing the right thing, then got to the business of what life requires you to do no matter what you are feeling. I had to move on in the midst of my confusion, pain, and sadness and find a place to live, a way to survive.

It didn't take long for the divorce to go through, one day in court and it was all over. I'm not sure what I expected, but Nicholas didn't even look upset. He looked blank and business-like. I tried to appear the same but I'm sure I failed miserably. My boss from Whole Foods was able to give me my job back at close to 40 hours a week and I now had my own apartment thanks to low-income housing and affordable food and childcare thanks to the federal government. I was resourceful when I had to be but I never *wanted* to be. Everyone seemed to cheer me on, Megan, Dad, even Mom wrote me and said I was doing the right thing. Amanda had allowed Abby and I to stay with her for a couple weeks and having a cheerleader at my side helped convince me that this scary path I had chosen of raising Abby alone, was the best thing for everyone involved.

There were moments I agreed with conviction and there were other moments, after Abby drifted off to sleep, that I wasn't so sure. Maybe if I had done something different, maybe he just needs to know what he's losing and he will change, then we could all be a family again.

37 - Eveline

My dearest daughter,

It is lonely here as Rachel stopped coming to visit me every Sunday and I haven't received a letter from you in a while. I know you must be very busy with everything going on in your life so I understand but I miss you. How is my beautiful little granddaughter? Is she crawling yet? Talking? I wish I could see her. I loved this age when you were little. I started teaching a GED class on Wednesdays under the supervision of Ms. Hampton and I love it. I really missed teaching and if feels good to be doing something.

I still have to work in the kitchen, which is really gross. I wake up at 2:30 a.m. and finish at around 11 a.m. and by that time I'm exhausted. I'm still in the same room with Terry and Jamie but things haven't been going so well lately. When I found out I was going to be teaching the GED class I was excited and shared the news with them but Jamie just started calling me names and making fun of me for being a 'kiss-ass' and 'teacher's pet'. Terry was happy for me. Jamie shoved me and out of defense I shoved back but after that I let her push me around because I didn't want to get into trouble. The guards came and split us up. I just want to maintain a good record so I can get out of this hellhole as soon as possible. I keep my bunk and personal space clean and I stay out of trouble. Most of the guards like me, and my counselor likes me so that is what matters. Enough about me. Are you okay? Have you found a place for you and Abigail yet? How is your job going? I was wondering if it's okay with your boss if you might be able to come out and visit me. I have put you on my list of approved visitors and I would pay for it so you wouldn't have to worry about that but I really need to see you. Let me know what you think. If you're not ready, I'll understand.

Love Always, Mom

38 - Rebecca

"She's still in daycare," I told Megan as I pulled into the apartment parking lot, "I got off work early which is good for my sanity but bad for finances." I wanted to stop by the apartment first and clean up a little before I picked Abby up from daycare. Nicholas will be coming over tonight to talk about Abby and to see her. I guess I want things to look nice, although I'm not sure why.

"Are you guys getting by okay? If you need anything, just let me know okay?"

"Oh I will, it's a lot of work but we're doing okay. Nicholas is coming over tonight to talk about Abby and some other stuff." I probably shouldn't have mentioned that particular tidbit.

"Well, that oughta be fun huh?" She laughed a little and I laughed back like *yeah, really* but in truth I was looking forward to it. I missed him and I missed being a family.

"It'll be fine, he hasn't seen Abby all week so it will be good for her too."

"Yeah, that's true, I guess. Becca, I can only imagine how difficult it is for you to be alone, especially with Abby." It was like she could read my mind. "But don't give in. Think of the big picture, all the things he's done and said for the last three years – even when you weren't married. The man will never change. It's always easy to be nice when you know you're not bound by anything."

"I know."

"I'm not trying to tell you what to do, it's your life, but you and Abby deserve someone who will adore you both and put you first in their life."

"Well, that's true!" I said, half joking and exaggerating, "I'm princess Rebecca, bubble baths and back massages every night!" I could break into tears right now if I didn't change the subject soon. "Hey Megan, before I let you go, I got a letter from Mom the other day."

"Oh yeah? Anything exciting?" Megan knew my Mom from when we were kids but she was even more shocked to hear about what happened than I was.

"Not really, just news about life in prison, asking about Abby and all that but she mentioned something in the letter that made me think. I'm not even sure why but it just struck me as odd all of the sudden. Maybe I've been watching too much Law & Order after Abby goes to bed! Anyway, she was saying how clean she keeps her bunk and personal space in her cell and of course she's always been that way; clean and organized I mean."

"Yeah?"

"Well, that day that it happened, Mom said that she had left the hammer out from hanging pictures the night before her parents arrived. That would mean that the hammer and supposedly the garbage bag were left at the bottom of the stairs the morning she picked them up, throughout the day and night and was there the next morning when she fell down the stairs. I don't know – it's just a little detail but it just doesn't seem right to me. Her parents are coming over – which she always stresses out about and wants everything to be perfect and she leaves a hammer and garbage bag out?"

"Interesting," I could hear Megan's wheels turning, "you know, now that you mention it, that does seem very out of character for her. Plus, didn't she say that she was hanging pictures of them up that weren't up before so that they could see them when they arrived?"

"Yeah, I think so."

"Well, you would think that she wouldn't leave the supplies out that she used to hang pictures with so they didn't say, 'oh you hang pictures of us up just before we come over huh?' It seems like that would be a little obvious."

"I guess it doesn't really matter much, except that if the hammer wasn't just lying out along with the garbage bag it would mean that she would have had to think about it more before she did it. She would have had to go get the hammer and bag which makes

the crime more . . . premeditated, as opposed to just an
uncontrolled moment of . . . what do you call it?"

"Disassociation, or something like that?"

"Yeah, that's it. Plus, that would mean she lied to me."

"Are you sure it doesn't matter?"

I thought about my mother, playing tag with me on the lawn,
teaching me how to cook, how to shave my legs. I pictured her
smiling and laughing. She seemed so different now. I still felt like I
was in the twilight zone and she would call me one day and things
would be back to normal. Maybe it did matter to me how it
happened. I wasn't really sure why I cared, but I have never
considered my mother mysterious up until now. I always thought
that I knew her like no one else did and that I understood her in a
way that no one else could. Maybe I don't understand her or know
her as well I as I thought. Just like I thought I knew Nicholas.

39 - Nicholas

I knocked on her apartment door, which felt beyond awkward. I missed Becca and Abby so I was really looking forward to the visit and hoping that somehow Becca would see me differently now that we were divorced. There was a part of me that enjoyed my freedom though. I had a chance to meet other people and go out and enjoy myself without having to explain my every move; for the most part anyway. I could tell that Becca still wanted me because it seemed like she just couldn't let go. Last week I stayed at my friend Nicole's house for the night because we had been out late with friends and I didn't want to drive home. Becca was jealous of my time with her and the fact that I took Abby to the petting zoo with her. I had the right to do whatever I wanted for God's sake! We are divorced! Becca showed up at Nicole's door at 7 a.m. with Abby in tow; I was astonished.

"You've got to be kidding me," I said coming out of the back room in just my jeans. "What the hell are you doing here?"

"I tried to call you a thousand times, where have you been?" She sounded on the edge of tears and disappointment.

"None of your business, you are my *ex*-wife, you can't tell me what to do anymore."

"Well, I need you to watch Abby today. Someone called in sick last night and I have to work in an hour!" Nicole was in the background in her sweats and a sexy hot pink camisole that was to die for which probably didn't help the situation.

"Okay, okay. Calm down," I said as I stepped outside and closed the door, "I'll take Abby and you can go to work."

"I am NOT giving her to you *now*. There is no way she is staying here with you and that little slut in there. Why don't you come to my house and you can watch her there."

I rolled my eyes and thought of how my day was just destroyed. I looked at Abby's innocent eyes and blooming smile. "Fine. I'll meet you there in ten minutes." I walked back in and slammed the door without saying another word.

She's been calling me all the time and we often get together to *talk about Abby* which often ends up with the two of us wrapped up in sheets and having pancakes together the next morning. I have to admit there are times I have called her and come over unannounced too, but in truth only when I had nowhere else to go.

Becca answered the door, somehow looking more beautiful than when we were married, "Hey Bec."

"Hey," she motioned me in and called to Abby playing with blocks on the floor, "Abby, honey daddy's here!"

40 - Rebecca

Now, when I'm on my own, I feel more confident and surer of the myself than I ever have before, but when he walks into the room, my defenses melt and I all I can do is stand there, naked and vulnerable. The more he moves on without me, the more I find myself clinging to him, clinging to the image of us as a family. I know I'm supposed to be the strong one *I'm better off without him, Abby needs a better role model* but is no role model better than one that needs polishing? Aren't we all human? Who crowned me queen of perfection? There are things that I need to work on too and I just think that we could be stronger together.

Both Megan and Dad have told me to stop depending on him so many times that it's starting to get annoying. They don't understand what it's like to be a single working mother, they don't understand what it's like to have to wake up and go to sleep alone while your ex-husband goes out to bars, has very little responsibility and sleeps with whoever he wants. He gets to see Abby every other weekend and sometimes during the week when I ask him to come over. He gets to be the fun parent with none of the daily responsibilities of teaching, guiding, disciplining, and caring for Abby. It just isn't fair. When do I get a break?

I wouldn't trade my time with Abby for the world and although I would never want to be where he is, sometimes I think for just one fleeting moment, that he got the better end of the deal. I guess part of me wants him back, not only because I still love him and want us to be a family, but because I want to even the playing field, to make it fair again.

Mom's friend and Power of Attorney had sent me money and a ticket to fly to Billings to visit her in the Montana Women's Prison. I had only been to Missoula while I was growing up so this would be new territory for me but I was thankful for the reprieve and, due to my confusion about Nicholas and I, I needed her guidance now more than ever. I arranged for Nicholas to watch Abby, which he wasn't too happy about because it meant that he had to be responsible for once. I left Denver behind for the time being and touched down at the Logan International Airport late in the afternoon. Everything was arranged and I felt like royalty. A car was already rented and was waiting for me when I arrived at the counter. They gave me directions to my hotel, conveniently located next to the mall. Billings was a small town compared to Denver so the drive to the prison wouldn't be too long.

I had already gone through the pre-approval process and had a list of the visiting hours and rules that I was required to follow during the visit. The next morning, I was more nervous than I thought I would be. I wasn't that nervous about seeing Mom, although I knew it would feel foreign, I was nervous about the process of going through the prison. I called Nicholas and Abby again in the morning and pried the reassurance out of him that I needed to hear. For as long as he has known me, sometimes I think he doesn't truly *know* me or what I need. Knowing someone that long and that intimately, some things should be intuitive.

41 - Eveline

I woke up earlier than I needed to. I wanted to sleep in so that the time would go by faster but I just couldn't contain myself. Today was the day I would get to see my daughter. I missed her more than words can say and it had been too long since I had seen her last. I tried to picture her over and over, how she might look years older and that motherly glow about her. I wished I could see Abigail but this is no place for a child and I would never expect Rebecca to bring her here.

Finally, after morning chores and afternoon lockdown it was visiting time and an officer came to escort me to the visiting room.

"Alright Kerner, let's go."

I had butterflies in my stomach all of the sudden worrying about what Rebecca would think, how she would react, seeing me in here. Everything looked worse when you were in prison. I've seen myself in the dusky Plexiglas and I know I don't look like I did when I looked in the mirror as a free person in my own bathroom. I focused on each step I took trying to make it as steady and confident as possible. I followed directions and the handcuffs were removed in a room just before entering the visiting room. As inmates, we called it the observation house or 'the house'. It was a huge room the size of a cafeteria sectioned off into quadrants with guards posted at each one and tables lined up in rows. There were vending machines off to the sides with everything from candy to chicken sandwiches and soda, and the visitors were not allowed to touch the inmates and vice versa. You felt watched as we all did every day at MWP (Montana Women's Prison). It was no different for the inmates, but for the visitors it was usually quite an adjustment.

As the guard unlocked the handcuffs, I looked up through a tiny window in the door to the other side of the house and saw her. She was an angel. Her brunette hair was softly curled and fell past her shoulders. She wore jeans and light blue polo shirt that complemented her womanly figure. She looked so grown up, had I missed that much already? My chest started to tighten, my heart beating faster with each passing moment and when the door opened, I called out to her, "Rebecca!" I had to hold myself back from running toward her so I didn't get in trouble with the officer escorting me. We met at our assigned table and I stood there for a moment hesitating but wanting nothing more than to hold her. Just then Rebecca flew into my arms weeping.

42 - Rebecca

The security guard quickly pulled us apart and instructed us to sit down. We dutifully obeyed and wiped our tears away both smiling in relief. We had six hours and somehow, we were able to talk up to the very last minute. I thought I would have trouble thinking of things to say but the words just flowed and the conversation felt natural. All she wanted to do was hear me talk, so for the most part I told her everything about my life, every detail about Abby and the apartment and my relationship or lack thereof with Nicholas and what I really wanted to happen between us. I confided in her and vented like I had never been able to do before. With Megan or Dad, I was always holding on to something, a piece of information that I could not divulge for fear of judgments but with Mom I didn't have to. I'm not sure if it was because she was in prison or if it was just her, but it didn't matter at that moment. It was what we both needed.

She understood my desire to be a family again and encouraged me to do what I thought was right for myself and for Abby. She said I should pray about it and I would know what to do. She had always been a spiritual person, but never very religious. Now that she was in prison, she was more spiritual than ever; writing prayer journals, participating in chapel activities, and analyzing the Bible as if she were the expert. There is a difference between being religious and being spiritual and I have to say that I don't really consider myself either one but right now I was open to any help I could get. We prayed together with Cheetos and M&Ms scattered around us as our time together came to a close.

It wasn't until the next day, my last visitation day, that I confronted her about the particulars of the crime that had plagued my mind. At first, I wasn't sure I should even bring it up but it wouldn't stop nagging at my conscience and I guess I just had to know.

"Mom, there's something I have to ask you," I took a deep breath, "I'm not quite sure how to say this and you don't even have to answer if you don't want to, but there's a piece that's missing and I guess I was hoping you'd fill in the blanks."

"I'll try, what's up?"

I told her, in more delicate terms, what I had told Megan. I told her that it wouldn't affect how I saw her just that I wanted to know because it just didn't make sense to me. She sat across from me; her body stiffening and her eyes went cold and gray. If she wasn't my mother, I would have been scared of what she would do next. Her eyes had a hint of moisture in them and then she spoke in a smooth, calm and calculated voice, almost like Nicholas would at times. It was a tone that made me pay attention while wanting to duck for cover at the same time.

"I'm not ready to talk about it Rebecca, can we leave it at that?"

It was as if she would break if I pushed any further and she was pleading for my help. I decided to let it go for now, giving her what she wanted. It seemed to be what she needed to be able to survive the next few minutes of our time together. I quickly changed the subject to Abby.

"Oh, I forgot to tell you Abby is starting to walk! I can't believe I didn't mention it before. She can't exactly walk yet but she grabs onto things and pulls herself up, her little legs wobbly and hesitant. She's brilliant!"

Mom smiled and her body relaxed again at my words. I watched her being escorted away from me, through the door to another world. I would soon have to walk into a new and foreign world of my own.

43 - Megan

"Counseling? Really? He agreed to that?" I can't believe it, after all she's been through, after all he's put her through, she wants to work it out with him?! He must be a damn good manipulator. Con artist is more like it. Bastard.

"I'm not saying we're getting back together Megan. I'm just saying we'll see how it goes. We're open to the idea, that's all."

"Becca, you've come *so* far. You work, you have a great job that has the potential to be a career, you just gotta hang on a little longer!"

"Actually, I had to turn down a raise last week and I don't think they liked that so we'll see how long they keep me around."

"What? Why?" What is she doing?

"Well, the raise would have put me 27 cents over the cutoff for childcare assistance. I did a lot of checking around and my day care would have gone from 20 dollars a month to 800! How can I come up with 800 dollars?"

"You're kidding me! That's ridiculous! How can they expect people to get ahead these days?"

"I know, it's insane. Well anyway it doesn't matter because Nicholas and I have been talking. Even if it doesn't work out between us, I'm sure he would help us out with some things if we needed. Honestly, I would love it to work out. I would love to be able to save this marriage."

"What marriage?" I had to stop myself from going down that road. It was as if she didn't care about the job, she was in a tunnel! "Well Becca, I can't say I'm happy for you or that I think it's the best decision to be completely honest. I think you're walking right back into the same life you just stepped out of, only this time you know what you're getting into." I couldn't help but allow some of my frustration to make its way into my words. I had to be honest with her.

"You don't know that Megan, you haven't seen him lately. He's changed so much since the divorce. It's not like I'm just taking his word for it. I've actually seen changes in his behavior. He's been putting me and Abby first lately and actually listening to me."

Well, good for him, after four years you finally put your wife and child first. Bravo! I continued as if I hadn't heard a word she said, "Only this time Becca you're bringing your daughter along for the ride!"

We argued for another 15 minutes, she justified everything he did and every decision she was making and I tried to make her see it differently.

"Don't you remember that just months ago you were telling me all these horrible things that he had said to you, how you felt like you were being *raped*? How do you just forget about that and go back to normal life?"

"Megan, he's not like that anymore."

Finally, I resigned myself to her decision, knowing that no matter what happened with counseling, she would go back to him. She said they would only get back together if at the end of a three-week counseling program, the counselor deemed them ready to be married again, but I knew differently. I don't think that even Becca really knew why she wanted to remarry him. She came up with all sorts of reasons; *I love him, we want to be a family, isn't it worth a shot if you can save a family, Abby needs a father.* None of those reasons quite fit.

She wanted him back because it was easier than the alternative. She was a struggling single mom with no skills because she put her dreams aside to make his come true. There were things she wanted to do that she couldn't do as a single mom or would be more difficult to do, like catering. It was easier in her mind to work at a relationship than it was to work at life and at raising a child with no breaks. I think to her credit she also really did cling to the image of a picture-perfect family. She wanted it all, even if it meant losing herself.

44 - Nicholas

"I'll take another," I called to the waitress as she whizzed by carrying twice her weight.

"So, tell me again what you said on the phone. What the hell's goin' on man?" Jason asked as he sucked down his second Miller Light. I called him and asked him to meet me here because of a phone call I had received from Becca. I didn't know what to do and I knew Jason would help me out, he was always there for me – we were like brothers and had been since we were kids. We struggled and partied through college together and now we worked together.

"She wants to get back together, like I said."

"As in, live together?"

"No, as in getting married again!"

"Woah! Are you kidding? I don't know what to say man, do you want to get back together with her?"

I shook my head in confusion, "I don't know what I want. On one hand I love being free to roam, you know? I love being able to come and go as I please without her nagging me about where I am or what I'm doing. But on the other hand, I miss her. I miss coming home and having her there, the smell of food cooking in the house, the sound of Abby playing. I miss that."

"I hear ya. What did you tell her?"

"I just told her I'd have to think about it." I thought of her surprised reaction and smiled a little. I didn't intend to; it was just my gut response but I think I threw her off a little. I think she thought because we were still involved off and on that I wouldn't think twice about taking her back.

"We're supposed to sit down tomorrow after she gets off work."

"Well, I'd take her back."

"What? What is that supposed to mean?"

"I'm just sayin' man, she looks a lot hotter than before. I don't know what it is, maybe it's because she's single."

I laughed, "Jason, you never change man…but she is hot, I'll give you that." We clinked our glasses and watched the rest of the game in silence on the TV in the bar. I thought about work and the empty house I would go home to. I thought about Becca and her long hair and sun-freckled face. Yes, we would remarry and this time I would never let her go.

45 - Rebecca

I hung up the phone, completely and utterly exhausted and walked onto the balcony so that I could feel the cold air sting my cheeks. I looked up at the gray and white swirls and closed my eyes, breathing in so deeply that my lungs burned. This way I could justify the tears running down my face, blaming the cold instead of my lack of emotional control. I am so sick and tired of being judged. Both Dad and my friends (all two of them) would tell me the same things over and over; how naïve I'm being, how dumb I am for wanting to go back to Nicholas and how he'll never change.

What gives any of them the right to tell me what I should or shouldn't do, whom I should or shouldn't love? How dare they. As if Dad has never made a mistake and then sacrificed everything to make it right again. As if Megan has never believed in someone she knew in her heart would fail, but did it anyway because she knew if she didn't give it a chance, she would regret it for the rest of her life. I just wanted to scream at the top of my lungs because during each one of these *pleasant* conversations it was like I wasn't even there, they talked right over the top of me, disregarding my opinions and feelings completely.

I just wanted my life back to the way it was, with the new Nicholas. He comforts me when I'm feeling like I have nothing left to give and just when my body can't take another moment without the touch of his hands, he's there. He's the only one who understands me. We need each other.

46 - Eveline

The stench of bleach burned my nostrils and tore at my skin but I didn't mind because now my outsides were matching my insides and at times like this, I almost felt comfortable in my own skin. Rebecca's words still ate at my heart like bleach corroding my fingerprints, tearing at my identity.

Just the notion that after all this time the events of that day still haunted her enough to make her question me. I hated that I was responsible for that. I am her mother. I should be the one to protect her from pain not be responsible for it. She's a strong woman and I have no doubt she will recover from what I've done, as will I one day, but knowing that I have added to her distress breaks me apart. I thought back to when Rebecca was five years old and her dad, Neil, and I took her to see the Grand Canyon. The trip was an attempt to reignite our marriage. Everyone does that; tries to leave their current reality hoping that the distance from their responsibilities will somehow bring them closer to each other. It's like putting a band-aid on a bruise. You can't see it anymore but the problem runs deep inside and the only thing that can fix it is time. Sometimes there's not even enough of *that* to make it disappear.

"Park here," I said anxious to take in the view. I turned around in my seat and winked at Rebecca, "You ready to see the biggest canyon in the world?"

"I was born ready." Neil always said that and I know it was meant to be funny but for once couldn't he think of something else to say? Annoyed, I ignored him and opened the back door to get Rebecca out of her car seat.

"I was born ready," she says copying her daddy. I rolled my eyes. She hopped out of the car, a ball of endless energy and vibrancy I wished I could bottle. I took her little hand with fingernails painted hot pink, and the three of us walked to the viewing point together. Thinking back on it now, I miss being one of three, a family for better or worse. Except that the *worse* won the fight, and the *better* became harder and harder to find as the years went on. The sun was a couple hours from setting, my favorite time of day because in the right conditions, the light makes everything look soft and golden. No words could describe the canyon's beauty and the three of us just stood there breathless and in awe of its enormity. Even Rebecca, who always had something to say, was speechless.

I turned to Neil, the golden light falling on his face and his eyes sparkling with moisture. He turned to me as if he knew I was taking him in and our eyes met with a strangeness that comes with a connection long overdue.

"Mommy, why can't we cross it to the other side?"

I told her that sometimes the gap is so wide and the canyon so deep that no bridge could connect the two sides.

47 - Rebecca

My second wedding day. Never in a million years did I ever think I would be getting married *twice*, especially to the same person. I still felt lonely and unsettled, informed by my family and friends that they would *not* be attending the wedding, out of protest for the whole situation. I had Abby and Nicholas, but secretly I would admit to myself that it wasn't enough. It felt like I had been abandoned on a day I should be allowed to celebrate. It was a simple wedding conducted by a local pastor in a church I had attended a couple of times. He knew some of our history and was one of the few people I knew that was in support of our decision to make this marriage work and keep our family together. The event was informal but sweet and I must say a lot cheaper than the first one!

Our honeymoon consisted of one night without Abby. We reconnected in a way that I didn't think was even possible. I felt like we had somehow bridged the gap that I had thought was too wide to cross, like the Grand Canyon. The connection felt fragile, made of rice paper or eggshells but I felt it, and that was all I needed to know. We had made the right decision. I clung to it and told Nicholas how good it felt to be his wife again.

I woke up early the next morning feeling refreshed and ready to take on my new life. I had lost my job at the store but I didn't care. Now I could spend more time with Abby, raising her myself instead of relying on some strangers at a day care to do the job. This was how it should be. I liked working but I wanted it to be flexible so that I could be here for Abby when I needed to be. I still wanted to try catering and maybe now was my chance to give it a shot like I was trying to do before things got so screwed up. Nicholas wasn't awake yet so I thought I would surprise him with a nice breakfast. As I was scrambling the eggs, his cell phone vibrated in his jacket pocket. At first, I didn't know what the noise was and ignored it. I opened the phone and noticed that he had a text message. *It better not be work calling him in, they know he requested today off.* It was a text message from Jenna! *Hey sxy, want 2 hk up?* What the hell was this? Tears welled up in my eyes as I though *what a way to start our new life together.* I blinked them back telling myself that there had to be a logical explanation and I would wait and ask Nicholas when he woke up.

He walked into the kitchen with a grin on his face from ear to ear. He gave me a good morning kiss and rubbed his stomach.

"Mmmm, it smells delicious Bec. I was gonna take you out for breakfast but this is even better!"

I guess I could have saved myself the trouble cooking – oh well, "Well, home cooked meals are always better right?"

After we had finished and we were clearing the table I told him about the text message. He was actually helping me clear the table, another example of how he had changed. I still couldn't get used to it but I liked it.

"You got a call earlier."

"Oh yeah? Who was it?" He reached for his phone and clicked through the menus.

We met each other's eyes and I didn't say a word. I just stared at him in a look that hopefully conveyed *I'm going to cry if you don't explain yourself.*

"Bec, look," he got up and walked over to me putting his hands on my shoulders, "Jenna and I messed around a little when you and I were divorced. We didn't even sleep together okay?"

"Why is she still calling you?"

"I haven't talked to her in like two months. I haven't told her that you and I are back together yet so she doesn't even know. I'll text her back and let her know. You have *nothing* to worry about okay? I married *you.*"

I smiled in relief; I knew there would be a good explanation. "Okay."

48 - Megan

"Megan, you're the only woman I know who would turn down an evening of drinks and men-bashing to spend time with her husband. You're a freak!"

"Yeah, I know. I'm crazy like that. See you guys next week!" I left work ready for my two days off. It took me three years of being a nurse to get the two days off in a row instead of having them spread out randomly throughout the week and it felt good. I thought of what she said and laughed to myself a little. I got that a lot from my friends and coworkers but it was true and there was no arguing with the truth. Oddly enough though, I learned to walk a thin line of being proud of what I had with Jeff and sympathizing with everyone else's misery because if I were *too* happy, I became the person no one wanted to associate with.

No one likes an overachiever or someone who has it *too* good because it makes them look bad, no one likes a happy person who is confident in themselves because it reminds people of what they don't have. Only my closest friends know who I am and respect me for it without judging me or without allowing themselves to feel insignificant because of who I am. They know that I've been at the bottom, that I know how it feels to be so lonely that you cut your skin just to feel something else. They understand that I, just like everyone else, have moments of my past I would rather not remember, moments I have overcome.

Why should I have to hide my happiness to make everyone else feel better? I never flaunt my life, especially when I talk to people like Rebecca who are enduring a painful situation. I know how it feels to watch someone else flourish while you just can't seem to catch a break and ache to just have one thing go right in your life. I would never purposely point out my successes with the intention of highlighting the failures of others.

I have been blessed – no, I got lucky. I am married to a man who holds my soul in the palm of his hand, a man that can finish my thoughts and make me laugh no matter how many years go by.

After years of not knowing what I was meant to do, I found a career that I'm passionate about and one that allows me to make my personal life come first and my professional life second. Until I found this career, I felt bored and suffocated, unable to allow myself the freedom to learn and grow.

One of my previous jobs was working at a department store for about a year, I think it was Mervyn's. I had the job down after about a month and would make up various tasks to keep myself from falling asleep like organizing the size stickers, cleaning the back desk, and drawing out customer interactions just so the day would go by faster. Other times, I would feel so intolerant of both customer and employee inabilities to understand what I felt were basic concepts. I either forced myself to be patient or I would go to the bathroom and cry in frustration, feeling trapped by everything around me.

This peace of mind that I have been lucky enough to discover has come at a price. Come to think of it, the price has always been there, it's just more obvious as I get older. In conversations with Becca, I hold back sharing with her something sweet Jeff said to me the other day, in nights out with girls from work I suppress my desire to leave early pretending I don't want to go home just yet. I have to be careful how positive I am about my life so that people close to me don't feel like they can't relate to me. I feel out of place so that other people don't have to.

It's not a bad price to pay really but I hate that I could make other people feel bad about themselves just by being me. I can tell when it's happening. Becca hesitates in mid-sentence, avoiding details she thinks I might judge her on, a co-worker skips over telling me she forgot to administer meds on a patient because she doesn't want me to think that she's incompetent, as if I judge everyone to my own standard *if you're not like me, it's unacceptable*. That's ridiculous! All I want is to be allowed to be who I am and for others around me to feel like they can do the same, no judgments passed. I guess I've always been an idealist.

49 - Rebecca

I still do a double take when I see Nicholas starting the dishes after dinner. He's been doing it pretty consistently since we got married. I start cleaning up like I always do, expecting him to make his way to the living room to watch golf or some other sports show but instead he has been moving to the sink as if he had been doing it his whole life. I stopped asking him to help around the house because he just does it. I considered it a miraculous transformation and I wasn't about to question such a thing. In my life, when something good happens I learned to accept it no questions asked because, well, it just didn't happen very often; up until now at least.

It was only after one special weekend that I dared to allow myself to accept my new beautiful life. I have the family I always wanted and my dream had actually come true. Could it be? He's been coming home for dinner every night and on the weekends, we always do something together. About six weeks after we remarried, we decided to take Abby to the carousel. We felt like she was old enough to enjoy herself and Nicholas and I used to go when it was just us, even though you rarely saw adults ride the horses without kids. It was the closest thing to flying I could think of and it made me smile every time I got on, even if I was in a bad mood. Abby obviously felt the same.

"Mommy, horsey!" she squealed in delight and giggled as the horse went up and down. Her wisps of dark hair fell across her forehead and flew straight up every time the horse rose.

"Wave to Daddy!" We both waved and smiled as he took a picture. I looked back at him fiddling with the camera and then looked down at our little girl.

"You know what kiddo? You're pretty good at this. You like the horsies?"

"Yeah, horsey!"

The carousel stopped and she started to whimper in disappointment, "I love you baby." She ignored me and cried as we walked away from the horses. I handed her to Nicholas for his turn and watched her smile return when she realized she would ride again.

As we drove home, the sun was setting over the mountains making the sky a brilliant gold and pink. I watched through the window and saw my reflection through the sunset and I thought *I'm happy*.

"Hey Bec."

I snapped out of my trance and glanced back at my daughter passed out in the back seat. "Yeah?"

"Remember when you mentioned you wanted to do that catering thing? It was a long time ago but I didn't know if you were still interested."

"Yeah, definitely. I just haven't had time, you know, with everything that's happened the last year. I obviously couldn't do anything about it when we were apart so it's just been on hold, I guess. I've only looked into it a little."

"Well, I have this thing at work. It would be really small, but I thought it might be something to get you started just to see if you like it."

"Wow! Really?" I couldn't believe my ears. Did I hear him right? Was he actually thinking about something for me that doesn't benefit him in some way? I pictured myself with a white apron directing people and distributing cookies and cakes and little hors d'oeuvres. "So, what's the job? When?"

"Well, it's next month and it would be for a meeting we're having with a big client from Salt Lake. Normally it wouldn't be catered but I might be able to persuade my boss to have you cater it since it will be relatively small and it might even impress the clients. He would probably just want little sandwiches and cookies or something, I don't know."

"Yeah, that would be great."

"I didn't want to ask unless you were serious so I thought I would ask you, see what you thought."

"Yeah, I'm up for it. Of course!" I tried to sound as excited as I could and although I was ecstatic at the thought of pursuing my dream, it also scared the shit out of me.

50 - Nicholas

"Mr. Evans, Mr. Manning, good afternoon gentlemen," I stood with my boss, Jerry, and three other members of my team as we greeted seven men that we were about to talk into signing on as a client of our firm. They were interested in building a new museum of science in Colorado Springs. They wanted a *cutting edge, contemporary, eclectic* design that would dazzle the public and bring people of all ages back into museums to learn about the history and future of science.

Before we began the meeting, Jerry wanted to butter them up a little and ushered them into a beautiful room adjacent to the conference room where Rebecca stood at a table covered with an astounding assortment of treats. The windows went from floor to ceiling and looked out onto the city. In the corner was a display of greenery and a small waterfall that fell over glass into a pool of bright blues and oranges. A few tall tables, stained a dark mahogany were set up with stools surrounding them giving the appearance of *stay, eat, but only for a little while, we don't want you to get too comfortable.* At the far end of the room there was a door that led into the conference room where the wheeling and dealing would happen.

Becca had been working on organizing this job since the day I got the okay from Jerry. It had consumed her and she juggled time with Abby and I to prepare for the event. Unfortunately, I had gone without a home cooked meal most nights since this all began. I guess I didn't really think things through when I offered her the opportunity. She said she cooked all day long just trying to perfect recipes that she didn't have the energy to put together a meal. So, we have been living off of various breakfast foods, Ravioli, macaroni and cheese, and hotdogs.

She stood behind the table now in a white buttoned-down shirt with a knee-high olive-green skirt. Her hair was tied back in a neat bun with strands of hair tucked behind her ears. My eyes wandered to the food as I watched the potential clients load up and compliment her on food they hadn't even tasted yet, but looked to delicious that they probably didn't have to taste it to know they would be back for seconds. She had made mini sandwiches held together by toothpicks; cracked wheat bread with smoked turkey, provolone cheese, salami, tomato, mayonnaise, and her specially handcrafted mustard (she refused to tell me what she did to it to make it so delicious). For the sweet tooth she had baked what she called buttered shortbread cookies and raspberry oatmeal bars; both made my mouth water and I have to admit she had a talent. I was dreading that she wouldn't be able to pull it off. She hadn't been able to pull everything together until the last minute, really, so I was starting to regret ever mentioning it to her.

"Maybe I can't do this. Maybe I wasn't cut out for this. I still haven't perfected the shortbread recipe and I have no idea what I can use to actually *serve* the food on." She was sweaty and the kitchen was a disaster with baking supplies everywhere; eggshells littered the counter and the sink, flour and sugar were everywhere and she looked like she was about to fall apart. I didn't know what to say. I was afraid she would make me look bad in front of my boss.

"Well, babe, maybe you shouldn't then." She stopped in her tracks; her fingers covered in dough, and threw her hands up in the air.

"What?! What are you saying? You don't think I can do it!"

"No – hey, I didn't say that. *You* said that. I am just saying, if you're that stressed out about it maybe you're just not ready, that's all." I was screwed no matter what I said at this point.

"You know what Nicholas, I've been working my ass off here and…" she trailed off and wiped her tears with her forearm, the only part of her body not covered in food, "…the least you could do is have a little faith in me."

Now here she was, everything together and even though she had to use the neighbor's Christmas platters, things had worked out okay and no one seemed to notice. I told her that it couldn't be obvious to the clients that we were married so when I went over to get some food I focused on conversation with my coworkers. I saw

Jerry look over at me and give me a thumbs up, so that was a good sign. Becca seemed calmer than I imagined her being given the prior nervous breakdown she had. Actually, as I looked at her from a table across the room, she appeared to move with such ease and natural comfort dishing out food, replenishing the platters and chatting with people that I was dumbfounded. She looked like she had been doing it her whole life. I could tell she was meant for it, like I was meant to be an architect. This should have brought me nothing but joy but I felt a twinge of jealousy, like she had taken something from me.

I held the door for everyone as they made their way into the conference room, their paper plates brimming with treats and their mouths full. I looked back at Becca and made eye contact with her just before I disappeared behind the door.

She held my gaze and I said, "You did great."

51 - Rebecca

"I know, it went better than I could have ever imagined. I really think I was meant for this."

"Sweetie I'm so proud of you, that's great news."

"The best part was that Nicholas really thought I did a good job, not that I need his approval or anything but it was for *his* boss so just that he thought I did great, says a lot because that means his boss liked it."

Mom had called me collect and it had been months since our visit so I was brimming with news and it was so good to hear her voice. We had been writing letters but she said she finally just had to talk to me.

"Since then, I have just been trying out some new recipes and slowly buying more equipment," there was silence for a moment, "but I think I might be doing a birthday party in a couple of weeks! I just have to talk to Bernice and make sure she still wants me to do it."

"That's good, I'm sure you'll do great. How is Abby?"

"Oh, she's great! She's so adorable and a little trouble maker ever since she became mobile. Now I can't keep up with her! I'll send you a picture of her soon."

"I talked to James the other day, actually he flew down to visit with Dad."

"Really?" I was a little surprised that her and James had spoken. I knew that he wanted to see her again but I didn't realize it would be this soon and I guess I just didn't expect him to be so…forgiving. It had been a horrible experience just as a daughter; I can't imagine what it would be like to know that your sister killed your mother. "Well, how did *that* go? Did you guys get along okay?"

"Actually, I feel really good about it. I was really nervous at first but we talked a lot about the past and how we felt. We also talked about what happened and he seemed to understand me. Of course, he had a hard time, as did I, but overall, I think we made some progress toward a relationship."

"Wow."

"Which is more than I expected. It was good to know I could still be part of the family."

"Yeah, I know what you mean. What about your dad, how did he take it?"

"He is getting older Becca, you know? He doesn't always know exactly what's going on but he cried when he saw me and -," she broke off holding back tears. I just gave her time. "He said he loved me and that he forgives me."

Now *that* is love. His wife of sixty-some years is dead at the hand of his daughter and he doesn't scream at her and ask her why, he doesn't berate her, he tells her that he loves her. I could only hope to be that kind of a parent. Not many people succeed at giving unconditional love. It's not that people don't want to, but sometimes other emotions get in the way like anger, pain, or the feeling of being used.

"James was telling me about the whole process of carrying out Mom's will." Her voice changed pitch and she went into business mode. I could always tell because she spoke with direction and purpose. I hadn't heard this from her in quite some time and I was taken aback by the confidence in her voice.

"Oh, that's right. I hadn't even thought of that. It's been a while I guess, is it already complete?"

"Not quite, since I obviously can't benefit financially from the death of my mother the money has to go somewhere so he's figuring all that out. He said it's possible that it might go to my beneficiary, which would be you."

"Really? That's kind of weird. You would think it would go to James or to your dad," I sensed a hesitation in her voice, "or whatever, I guess we'll find out."

"Well, if you do get the inheritance Rebecca, I would expect you to help me out with things when I get out."

"What?" Was I hearing her right? She was a long way from getting out of prison, why even discuss it.

129

"I'm going to need a car and a place to live. It's the least you can do."

"Mom, hold on here. You are talking about me giving the money to *you* after *I* have inherited it because it is *illegal* for you to inherit it. Are you asking me to give the money to you?"

"No! Of course not Rebecca, I'm just saying that as my daughter I would expect you to be there for me like I have been there for you. You wouldn't go buy a $400,000 home, would you? Because that would just be a waste of money if you ask me."

"Mom, this is ridiculous!" I was pacing around the length of my house making exaggerated hand gestures that no one could see. Abby, however, was enjoying the entertainment. "You've got to be kidding. First of all, I am not going to break any laws just because you think you deserve the inheritance. Secondly, we don't even know if that money will end up with me or not, so just give it a rest, okay!" I stuttered over my words and adrenaline was pumping through my veins. It was one of those situations where someone says something to you that completely throws you off kilter and you don't have the confidence or the skill to put together an intelligent, witty response, so you just spit out the first words that come to mind, whether it was what you wanted to say or not. It is only *later* that you think of how you really wanted to respond, with all the perfect words put together in the perfect way to get your point across.

"Rebecca, I only have 15 seconds left so I gotta go. I love you so much! It was really great talking to you. I'll write soon."

"I -," then she was gone, replaced by a dial tone. My mouth was open in disbelief. I spoke out loud to myself, to Abby, to anyone listening.

"Who *was* that? What is she, bipolar? Oh my God! Did I really just have that conversation?" I looked over at Abby sitting on the living room floor playing with her stuffed ponies and started laughing.

"Were you enjoying yourself? Huh?" Abby just giggled in agreement.

I guess I was a fool to think that she could actually be a normal mother, one with no strings attached. It was always something wasn't it? Why should this be any different? There was the time she bought me a little car right out of high school, but after having it for six months she took it away from me because I wasn't using it to drive *only* to work. The year after that a friend from out of state was flying in to visit (a ticket purchased by her). She cancelled the flight using *my* name without me even knowing about it. I found out when my friend had called to tell me her flight was cancelled. I can't even remember now why she cancelled it. It could have been that I wouldn't go visit her for Easter or something. She was always pulling the rug out from underneath me if she didn't get what she expected out of the deal, but for some reason I kept going back for more.

I have always given her another chance because that's what families do. It's an unconditional love, or it's supposed to be. I thought things would be different after she went to prison, that maybe now she would stop taking things for granted. We had such a great visit and she was so supportive of my life and the decisions I was making. Then out of nowhere, bam! The ulterior motives finally made their presence known. So, this is what you *really* care about. How foolish I was to think otherwise.

52 - Eveline

We were in the checkout line at Safeway and Neil and I were in the middle of a fight, the same fight we always had that never ended; just picked up where it left off the last time. I was multi-tasking as always, trying to pay for the groceries and watch Rebecca while he was standing off to the side waiting for me to finish. *No really, I got it.* I grabbed the cart full of bagged groceries and pushed it with as much force as I could trying to make my anger as obvious as possible. We resumed our conversation and after putting the groceries in the car I looked around feeling like something was missing. I briefly ran through my shopping list as Neil looked at me. *What?*

Rebecca! I had forgotten my own daughter. I ran back into the store with Neil at my heels. I looked everywhere for her, interrogated the checker where we had just come from and I ran by every isle of the store looking down each one in hopes that I would see her. I was panicked and lost without her.

When I got back to the front of the store I was in tears and ready to lose it when I saw Neil holding her hand by the customer service desk next to the bubble gum and candy. I smiled at Rebecca, shot a jealous glance at Neil and said, "Let's go."

53 - Rebecca

"I feel really bad about going, are you sure?"

"I'm sure, go have a night out with the girls. How long has it been Bec?"

"Okay, you have a point there."

"They'll be here any minute, you better get crackin'."

"Okay, okay." Sheesh, push me out the door why don't you. We *have* been spending a lot of time together so I guess he's probably getting a little tired of me. He probably can't wait for a little time to himself. I have to admit I was yearning for a little 'girl time' myself. It's been ages since I have been able to go out and have some drinks and maybe see a movie - since before I had Abby.

I took one last look in the mirror. I wore my favorite jeans and a black frilly button-down shirt that I hadn't worn in years. I wouldn't say I was comfortable but that's exactly what made me feel good. I felt like a woman instead of a housekeeper. I was attractive when I put myself together right. A little curvy in the hip area but a few curves never hurt anyone. It was better than being one of those anorexic looking girls that you see nowadays with their jeans down to their ass-crack and their shirts up around their ribs leaving nothing to the imagination. You can even tell what kind of underwear they have on at a glance. Why bother?

Tonight, I planned on being myself for a change and relaxing a little with a couple of women I had come to know via library story time. Come to find out we had a lot in common, so we started hanging out a little more. Tracy would bring her little boy over or Jen and I would go for walks. We haven't known each other very long but we all had fun together and have been planning this night for two weeks.

"Okay bye! Have fun!" Nicholas stood in the doorway with Abby waving her little hand at me as we drove off.

"He seems so sweet Becca," commented Tracy. This would be the first time she had actually met Nicholas and I had not told either of them our rocky history. All they knew was that we have been married for a few years (I fibbed a little there).

"Well ladies, shall we put on a little music?" We all yelled and began our night of freedom.

After we grabbed a bite to eat at Applebee's, we headed off to a small bar across the street. It was a very tasteful bar since none of us wanted to go to the places our husbands dragged us, the type of bars where you inhale smoke all night and are surrounded by guys that stare at you as if you were naked and by women who don't care who they go home with. We went to a place called Martini's Place and I loved it the moment I walked in. There were couches set up around coffee tables and the bar stools looked like they were originally from a 50's diner. It was cozy and lively, just what I needed.

"Here's to us!" We clinked our glasses and sipped our drinks while we told funny stories about our children and our simple little lives. Just then I spotted a vaguely familiar face.

"Jack?" I whispered, staring off into the crowd.

"Becca? You all right? You stopped in mid-sentence you know."

I came to my senses, "Oh, I – sorry. What was I saying?"

Jen wasn't going to let me slide, "Oh no, you don't get out of it that easy!" She leaned in to the center of the table, "Who's Jack?"

"Right there," I pointed him out sitting at the bar with a girl, "I can't believe it's him. I, well, we met on a plane. I was flying back from a funeral in Boston and we talked on the way back that's all, nothing special. It's just that I haven't seen him since then. It's been a couple years I guess."

"Oh, well he's hot," said Tracy fanning her face.

"I think you should introduce us Becca."

"Yeah, go talk to him."

"Are you guys crazy? No way, he's obviously with someone. I wouldn't want to intrude or anything."

"It's not like you're asking him out, just a friend saying hi to a friend, right?"

God, he looked good. He moved with such ease. I forgot how a man could be intriguing without being charming. Charming always got me into trouble and it never lasted. It *would* be nice to say hi to him at least.

"Okay." I took another swig of my screwdriver and hopped off the chair.

"Whoohooo!" they shouted in unison. I looked back and shushed them promising an introduction.

I approached him from the side and smoothed my hair just before he looked my way. His eyes sparkled and his body changed shape as soon as he recognized me. I could almost feel his heart pounding with mine as I stood across from him and smiled. *Say something Becca.*

"Jack, right? I – hi – Becca." I put my hand out not knowing what else to do or what the proper greeting should be. "I don't know if you remember me but –."

"How could I forget?" We stood there, hands locked, for what seemed like an eternity, then the woman I assume was his date, cleared her throat jolting us out of our trance.

"Yes, Becca, this is my girlfriend Julie. Julie this is Becca, we met on a plane ride a couple of years ago and well, it's just a nice surprise. It's been a long time."

Julie put out her hand and I shook it. It was one of those weak girly handshakes; I hate those. "Nice to meet you Julie."

"So, how have you been Becca?"

I didn't dare tell him my horrific humbling life story, "Oh things are great. Actually, I had the baby – of course," I must have been blushing, "she's almost two now and she's just adorable, we named her Abigail - Abby." I noticed Julie relaxed a little after I mentioned Abby. "Nicholas and I are doing great."

"Oh, good."

"How about you? What's new with you?" I was desperate to change the subject.

"Well, I got a promotion at work. I am now a senior copyrighter for the Denver Post!"

"Baby," Julie cooed, "oh my God!"

"I was gonna tell you tonight, that's why I figured we would go out and celebrate."

I felt like I was intruding on a moment that should have been just between them. "Wow, Jack that's great! Good for you." I couldn't help leaving a trace of regret in my words. It wasn't jealousy. I wanted nothing more than for him to succeed and be happy, it was simply that I hadn't done a whole lot with my life. It was shame more than jealousy. "I'll have to read the paper more often!" We all laughed dutifully.

"How long have you guys been together?" I noticed there were no rings on their fingers but I couldn't help but ask the question.

"Jack and I have been together three months and four days."

"She could probably give you the hours and minutes too." Jack smiled and Julie gave him a playful shove.

"Well, Nicholas's job is going well, he just got a new client for a museum that is supposed to go in Colorado Springs. Did I ever tell you he was an architect?"

"No. What about you?"

There it is, the dreaded question. *What about me? I'm a loser and that's pretty much the whole story*. I stole a quick glance back at Jen and Tracy. "Well, not too much in that department really, I take care of Abby."

"Hey that's a lot of work taking care of a kid. Don't down-play that!"

All of the sudden I remembered my catering. *Hello! Earth to Becca!* "Oh, well, actually I have been working on something. I'm trying to get into catering. So far I've only done a few jobs but I really love it and my food is pretty good."

"Wow, that's great," Jack was grinning from ear to ear and I had to look away, "that suits you. I could see you as a caterer."

"Really? Well, that's the goal but it'll take some time." I felt like my time was running out and I took the out. "Oh, I'm here with my friends," I pointed toward Tracy and Jen and they waved anxiously back, "they wanted to meet you if you don't mind. It will just take a second."

Julie looked confused but Jack stood up right away, "Sure, honey I'll be back in a second okay?" He kissed her cheek and left her at the bar.

I led the way to our table and introduced him. I introduced Julie from a far just to put her at ease. I know I would feel uneasy if my boyfriend were over at a table full of girls without me. We talked for a few moments and I walked with him toward Julie but stopped halfway.

"Well, it's so good to hear that things are going well for you. Julie seems really nice."

"Yeah, she is. You too, I'm glad things are going okay and I bet your daughter is beautiful, like you. I'd love to meet her one day."

A silent sadness filled the space between us.

"Are you sure you're okay?" He asked.

I looked down at my feet then up at him. *How did he know that there was something missing, a piece of myself that I couldn't quite place?*

"Yeah, I'm okay. It was really good to see you again Jack." I turned to walk away, afraid that if I stayed any longer, I would find it.

"It was good to see you too Becca."

54 - Nicholas

Finally, peace and quiet. I swear we've been joined at the hip these past few months and it's driving me crazy! Can't a guy get a little space once in a while?

"Well Abby, it's just you and me kiddo. I think it's bed time, what do you think?"

"Night-night?"

"That's right! Night-night time." I grabbed her playfully and threw her up in the air a few times. This was her favorite thing and I loved doing it because it got her giggling uncontrollably. I read her a Dr. Seuss book, the shortest one I could find, and put her to bed. We would have to get her a toddler bed soon. She was growing up so fast!

Just as I sat down to watch the season premiere of Desperate House Wives, my cell phone rang. This is something I would never admit to my friends but hey - the women are hot. Damn, can she not survive without me? She's probably checking up on me. I wasn't going to answer it but then I thought maybe she was checking on Abby. I hopped up off my chair and hit the mute button to the TV.

"Yeah?"

"What are you wearing?"

"What?" No way could that be Becca I had to hold the phone away from me to look at who was calling, Jenna. I haven't heard from her in close to a year since I told her to stop calling.

"I miss you Nicky. I'm lonely."

"Well, that sounds like a personal problem."

"No, I think it's *your* problem, why don't we solve it together? Your wife isn't home right?"

"Look Jenna, as much as I would love to help you out with this little problem you have, it's not a good idea." Just as I sat down in my chair again, I heard a knock at the door. Shit, what now. "Hold on, someone's at the door."

I opened the door, ready to send whoever it was away so that I could enjoy my TV show, when I saw her. Her short blonde hair was in curls and her cell phone to her ear.

"Honey, I'm home." Her eyes were dark and sensual. She flipped her phone closed and slid her finger down the front of her coat pulling it open to reveal her body underneath. I stood there, dumbfounded with my cell phone and my mouth still open.

Underneath her long black coat, she wore the sexiest underwear I have ever seen in my life. The pink lacey bra barely contained her breasts and the matching underwear was see-through leaving nothing to the imagination and everything to be desired. I dropped my phone and was just getting ready to tell her that she should really go, when she stepped up into the house with her sparkling silver stilettos and without a word pushed me against the wall kissing me hard. I felt myself harden and after my initial shock I gave in and put my hand underneath her coat touching her smooth soft ass. Hmmm, a thong, something Becca wouldn't be caught dead in. Jenna kissed me harder and shut the door with her silver heel.

55 - Rebecca

I lifted the trunk and took stock of my supplies. This would be my third job as a caterer. I can't believe I can actually call myself a caterer. I still feel like I don't know quite what I am doing but I get through it every time. It has started to give me a sense of pride in who I am like I have never felt before. The pride I feel when I look at Abby is wonderful but it's very different from this; they each satisfy a different side of me. Each client has loved my food and has requested my service just from hearing about me from a friend. I haven't had to do any advertising so far which has saved me a lot of money. Pretty soon, my kitchen won't be big enough to serve the purpose. I'm surprised the oven hasn't burst into flames by now! This event is a birthday party for the eight-year-old daughter of one of the bigwigs at Nicholas's firm. Nicholas said he's never met the guy, which I was thankful for because if something went wrong, I didn't want him to connect it to Nicholas.

Her name was Kayla and she wanted the theme of her party to be Prom Barbie. Needless to say, I had to do a little research and ask lots of questions. Come to find out Prom Barbie always wears red, rides in a red limousine, and attended the prom with none other than Ken! I picked the cake out of a book and it was the first 3-tier cake I had done but it turned out beautifully. It should, I must have made the cake three times before I made the *real* one. It was a lot of work but none of my *trial treats*, as I called them, went to waste. I would always give some to neighbors, send some with Nicholas to work, or give samples to Tracy and Jen. At the top of the cake, instead of Barbie and Ken, was a red limousine. The father, Rick wasn't ready to think of his little girl in a wedding dress just yet and he said it was just too similar to a wedding to have a cake topper like that. This is when I suggested the red limousine and he said the idea was brilliant. I was *brilliant*!

I walked over to the cake table to set up and noticed that all of Kayla's friends were running around dressed up in various mini prom dresses. There were even a couple of boys dressed in tuxedos, yanking at their collars. Kayla, of course, was the only one in a red dress looking like a princess, like Prom Barbie.

With the cake, I served little balls of chocolate and vanilla ice cream the size of a large marble with shavings of red chocolate on top. I also had bowls of white chocolate-dipped strawberries placed strategically around the tables. These appeared to be a big hit with the adults.

Just as the last of the kids ran from the table with their cake my cell phone vibrated in my apron pocket. I pulled it out briefly to check the caller ID but I noticed Rick walking toward me at the same time. It was Nicholas calling to see how things were going. Well, I would just have to call him back; I'm working.

"Hi Rick!" I replenished a few bowls of strawberries.

"Hey Becca, you're a hit! Kayla loves you and everyone keeps giving me compliments on the food which, of course, is all your doing so I thought I would come pass the compliments on to you."

"Well, thank you so much! Kayla is a delight and the kids look like they're having fun."

"She especially liked that you wrote her name on each tier of the cake!" We both laughed. Around the sides of each tier, I had written in red icing *Happy Birthday Kayla.*

"Yes, I thought that would be a nice touch."

"Well, after they're finished eating, we'll probably open presents and then try to wind the party down a little for the sake of the parent's sanity!"

"I understand! I'll just be here until everyone goes inside then I will pack up."

"Here you go." He handed me a check for 300 dollars and I couldn't help but smile. "You deserve it! Thanks a lot Becca, I'll be recommending you to my friends."

"I appreciate it Rick, thank you!"

A few more kids came back for seconds and then everyone trickled inside for the opening of the presents. *Not too bad Becca.* Another one down! I was putting the last of my supplies into the car when out of the corner of my eye, I saw a woman running toward me waving her arm. Oh God, hopefully she wasn't going to complain. The day had gone so well.

I smiled on the outside and winced on the inside, "What can I do for you?"

"Hi, sorry to wave you down like that but I wanted to catch you before you left. My name is Angelina Romero Lopez," she put her hand out and I introduced myself in return, "I just loved your cake! The whole display was just beautiful."

I sighed a quiet sigh of relief, "Oh, thank you so much."

"Well, I'm getting married to my fiancé Eddie in about four months and I've been looking for a caterer. We had one but, well, it's a long story that I won't bore you with but the bottom line is I was wondering if you might be interested?"

I could barely contain myself. Are you kidding? I was actually being asked to cater a wedding! I tried to avoid appearing overly excited, as I didn't want to scare the poor woman off. "I would *love* to!"

"Oh great! Oh, Eddie will be thrilled. He loved the strawberries."

"Yes, they seem to be a favorite."

We stood there in silence for just a moment until I remembered myself, "So! I guess my next question is when can the two of you meet to discuss the details of your wedding?"

"Yes! That would be great, um, Eddie and I both have weekends off. I teach grade school so anytime on the weekend."

"Okay, well, how about next Saturday at one?"

"Great! Rebecca it was so good to meet you, I'm glad I caught you."

"Please call me Becca. It was a pleasure meeting you too! I'll see you Saturday!"

"Okay," she turned and practically skipped as she made her way back to the house.

She was one of the most beautiful women I have ever met. Beautiful in a natural, humble sort of way that left you wanting to know more about her. What I liked most was that she didn't speak to me like a servant. Some people seem to think that because I'm their caterer they can order me around but she came across like we were colleagues working on a project *together*. That's the way it should be. She was so personable and comfortable in conversation that I didn't even feel nervous, for now anyway. Wait till I tell Nicholas about this. I'm going to cater a wedding!

56 - Nicholas

I flipped the cell phone shut in frustration. Where the hell is she? I've called her twice and she's not answering which is not like her at all, usually she answers my call on the first or second ring. I know she's catering a birthday party today but how long can it take? I thought she would be done by now. I've been out golfing with Jason most of the day and was on my way to Blockbuster against my better judgment. Becca wanted to rent a movie tonight and watch it after we put Abby to bed, but I had no idea what she would want to see. Well, besides a chick flick and I wasn't about to go there. There had to be something we would both enjoy.

The more I thought about it, I wasn't so sure about this whole catering thing. I know I was the one who convinced her to do it but I guess I never thought it would go this far. I thought it would just be like a hobby, something to keep her occupied, but it is practically turning into a full-time job. I grabbed something out of the new release section, paid the cashier and headed home hoping she would be there when I arrived. I thought about how she lit up when she was doing her first job at my office. I know she must love doing it just as I love what I do. I didn't want to get in the way of that because I know what it's like to find something you can identify with but it was starting to take away from us.

I had talked to Jason about it today and we both agreed that a woman's place should be primarily at home, with the kids. Unless, of course, there is a financial need but I'm providing all that she needs so there is really no reason to make catering her full-time gig. Lately we've had Abby in day care or being watched by friends and I've gone along with it so far but I really feel that Abby needs her mother. Maybe I would talk to Becca about it tonight. I'm sure when she heard my point of view she would understand. She loves spending time with Abby and I know she hates to leave her.

As I approached the house, I saw her car in the driveway and smiled. *Yes!* She had the trunk open and was lugging a box from the car into the house. She turned around to use her hips to push the door open and looked up to see me come into the driveway. She nodded and smiled in recognition and attempted to wave but lost control of the box and almost dropped it.

I laughed as I hopped out of the truck and grabbed the movie. I almost walked past her open trunk but noticed one box of supplies left so I lifted it out and closed the trunk.

"Hey Bec!"

"Hey you! How are you?" She gave me a kiss. Evidently, she was in a particularly good mood. "I picked up Abby on my way, she's in the playpen in the living room."

"Oh, okay. I'll go say hi." She closed the door and watched me play with Abby for a little while. "So, how was your day?"

"It went so great! Everyone *loved* the cake and the adults loved the strawberries as predicted."

"They're one of *my* favorites too."

"And, you'll never guess what happened just as I was about to leave!"

"The birthday girl threw up."

"No, crazy! Actually, this lady came up to me and asked me to cater her wedding! Can you believe that? I'm actually going to cater a wedding. It's in about four months and I meet with her next weekend to talk about the specifics."

"Wow," I said not enthusiastically enough, "that's good news for you. Great."

She didn't appear to notice the lack of excitement in my reaction as I had hoped, instead she went on to tell me more details than I wanted to know about Kayla's birthday party. The evening ran on and finally the moment came when Abby was in bed and we could have a conversation without having to care for her at the same time.

Becca was wiping kitchen counters, picking up toys and clothes off the living room floor, and clearing the kitchen table of random items that had made their way there.

"Bec, can we talk?" She made quick eye contact with me and I suddenly realized that I had worded that wrong. That intro made it sound like I had something I was hiding and I quickly let her know. "It's nothing major, I just wanted to talk about your catering that's all." Her body relaxed. Jenna's smooth curves briefly filled my mind.

"Okay, sure. What's up? Do you have something going on next weekend?"

"No, I just – well I've been thinking about this catering thing and I'm not sure it's a good idea for you to allow it to consume you as much as it has."

"What are you saying?"

"Just hear me out for a second. I'm worried about Abby. She hasn't had as much time with you because you've become so busy with catering. You're never here and things at home are suffering. Besides I want to be able to see you during the time that I *do* have off. I'm just saying that it's become almost a full-time job and I don't think it's the appropriate time for that right now." There, now she had to understand where I was coming from. It was a valid point after all.

"That's not fair Nicholas." Her voice was shaky but she was holding it together. "How can you ask me to give this up? You were the one that said I should follow my dream!"

"Yeah, I know but I didn't think it would take off like it has."

"Oh, thanks for the vote of confidence."

"No, I just mean that I thought we discussed the catering being fine as long as it didn't take away from Abby or our home and now it is doing just that and it's just not appropriate!"

"I can't just *stop*! I have commitments that I have to honor. I know you don't know what it's like to stand behind your promises, but I refuse to let these people down!"

"Is there something you haven't told me?" Why did she not want to let this go? Was there something else or someone else?

"What are you talking about? No! I have this wedding to do at the very least. I can't just call her up and say 'sorry I changed my mind, good luck finding another caterer'! You have no reason NOT to trust me."

"Well, you sure don't want to let it go so what am I to think?"

"You are 'to think' that I follow through with my commitments and that I love what I'm doing right now. You are 'to think' that you shouldn't expect anything less of me than for me to do the right thing."

"First of all, *you* don't tell me what I'm supposed to think. Second of all, our daughter needs you and whether it is now or in the *very* near future you will take this catering thing down a notch or two or I will make sure that you never get another job again." She drives me crazy sometimes! Why does she push me to the point where I have to force the issue? Why can't she just understand and go along with it? I had to get out of the house, just for an hour or two. I was feeling suffocated, my lungs aching and my head pounding.

I grabbed the keys, "I'm going out. I'll be back in an hour or so."

"Nicholas you can't just walk out –." I slammed the door cutting her off. I didn't want to hear anymore. I just drove until I saw the sweet neon lights of the casino.

57 - Rebecca

I turned down the music so I could think. Sometimes, driving was the only time I could really collect my thoughts; just me and some music or silence was all I needed to sort things out. The meeting with Eddie and Angelina went very well. Their wedding would be beautiful, a picture-perfect event, and I was excited to be a part of it. There was a jealousy though, in the back of my mind at the fact that they were made for each other. My first wedding was everything I wanted on the surface but Nicholas had turned it in to a drinking party (starting before the ceremony) and the air was heavy around us with tension. I knew in the back of everyone's minds they didn't want the wedding to happen but no one said a word. Why was it so hard for us and so easy for everyone else?

I felt even more committed to catering after my meeting with Angelina and I just couldn't connect why Nicholas wanted me to give it up when he had to know how much I loved it. I thought about how things used to be with me only working once in a while, home most days, especially for dinner. I always had it on the table shortly after he got home. After Abby was born, I was home even more. Suddenly it occurred to me. He doesn't like not knowing. It's not that he doesn't want me to be happy, maybe it's that he is losing control. This made me smile a little; I couldn't help myself. It's good for him to have to lose a little of that once in a while; then again it seems like I lose either way. My smile disappeared and my eyes started to fill.

If I decrease or completely stop catering, I lose a part of myself and I lose this blissful feeling of pride, accomplishment, and satisfaction. If I keep catering, my life will become a living hell. I'm not stupid, despite what Megan thinks, I have not forgotten who Nicholas has the ability to become and I know I don't want to live like that. Things have been so great between us and I don't want to jeopardize that. Damned if I do, damned if I don't. That's wonderful. I let the tears roll down while I still had the opportunity to let myself go. No one could see me. No one could judge me and probe me with questions about why I was crying. At least I had that.

Four months went by quickly and for the most part, we both avoided the conversation about catering. I had no idea what I would do but to keep things from exploding I placated him with the notion that this would be my last event. I didn't make any promises but I had to tell him something. I was secretly looking forward to this wedding with every fiber of my being, especially if this would be my last job. The preparation was a little trickier this time. I was careful about when I practiced baking and made sure that I had dinner of some kind on the table when I could.

While he was at work, I would sometimes have the neighbor watch Abby for a couple of hours while I picked up more supplies or put together a prototype cake. Sometimes Abby and I would do it together. While I practiced cake decorating on tin foil, she would eat roses and stars and paint with the colors loving every minute!

Finally, the day came. I loaded my car the night before and had rigged a special device in the car that would allow me to transport the cake without a disaster. I went to leave early in the morning dressed in black pin-stripe pants, a white button-down shirt and my apron under my arm.

"Okay, I'm off! Wish me luck!" I kissed Abby and leaned in to kiss Nicholas.

"Where the hell are you going this early in the morning?" You're kidding me, right? Do you *never* listen to a word I say?

"Babe," I laughed nervously, "I'm going to cater that wedding I've told you about a million times, remember? You said you would watch Abby today."

"I never said that."

I was about to have a nervous breakdown. "*Yes*, you did!"

"Becca, I have plans with Jason today."

"No, you don't." This cannot be happening. Does he really not remember? "You can cancel your plans with Jason, otherwise our daughter will be by herself because I am going to this wedding right now that I have been working on for four months and that you have known about the *whole* time!"

"Fine, I'll cancel my plans. But this is the last time Bec, I'm done bending over backwards for you when I don't get anything in return."

"I really don't have time for this conversation. I have to go. I'll call you when I'm done."

I used the time in my car to calm myself down and to switch gears. I gave myself a little pep talk. *I need to focus on this wedding. I just have to get through the day. It's going to be an amazing wedding because you are an amazing caterer!* It seemed to be working. Everything else disappeared as soon as I stepped out of my car and on to the grass of the Denver Country Club. I've never seen anything so beautiful; the blue main building with white trim, stone bridges, flowers, and green grass. It was paradise and a wonderful place for a wedding. I checked in with the wedding planner and she went over the schedule with me, and where I would be setting up. She had every detail down to hours and minutes on her clipboard. She was a genius and I took notes.

My world was transformed for the day and I got to work right away. There was a lot more food this time than at my previous events so I had a lot to do and when that's the case, four hours is not a lot of time! Angelina had not made me responsible for the dinner (which I told her I would not be able to do anyway) but made my specialty, the cake and various hors d'oeuvres, which I was very proud of. The day flew by without a hitch and before you know it, I was packing up and preparing to leave. I thought before I took off, I would take advantage of the beautiful scenery and walk around the country club grounds.

Before I could escape, Angelina and Eddie found me, breathless from dancing the night away.

"You guys look so beautiful! Congratulations!"

"Becca, we can't thank you enough for everything! The food was wonderful and beyond our expectations. You have a God-given talent you know."

"Well, I appreciate the compliment. Thank you for choosing me and allowing me to be a part of your beautiful wedding. Your planner is a genius!"

"I know! That was Eddie's find, right baby?"

"That's right!"

"Well, we just wanted to make sure the wedding planner paid you and you had everything you needed before we head off to the Bahamas!"

"Yes, I just got the check from her, thank you. Listen, you guys have a wonderful time in the Bahamas and soak up some sun for me!" I couldn't survive this conversation any longer without sounding bitter. Some friends had begun pulling the newlyweds back to the dance floor.

"Okay, well thanks again!"

"You're welcome, bye." I waved as they were being dragged away giggling with joy.

I closed the trunk and sighed in disappointment of the day ending, knowing that I would have to go home. A walk would do me some good before I headed back into the fire. I might as well take advantage of a little serenity while I can. I'll call Nicholas after. I made my way past the main building's white pillars, down the stone path, across the grass covered stone bridge and onto the golf course. I walked along the side just in case there were a few people on the course taking advantage of the last of the golden evening light. Amidst the sound of birds chirping and water trickling in a stream nearby, I heard soft footsteps behind me and turned to see if it was my imagination.

"Are you Rebecca Mitchell?" A woman about my age, with a round figure and beautiful auburn hair approached me waving.

I waited for her to come closer, "Yes, that's me."

"You're the caterer for the wedding, right?"

"Me again, what can I do for you?"

"I'm Hannah Bean, a friend of Tracy's, she said I might find you here today." I must have looked a little confused at why she was at the wedding because she continued quickly, "I'm also a colleague of Angelina's at the school; we're both teachers."

"Oh! Okay, wow – a small world I would say!" We shook hands and exchanged stories, finding more and more in common as we spoke. "Would you like to join me? I was just taking a short walk, enjoying the scenery."

"Sure, it's beautiful."

We ended up walking for over an hour. It turns out that she also has a daughter about Abby's age and a love for cooking but has never really followed through and done anything with it. She proposed gingerly that maybe we could work together; especially on the big jobs like weddings and such as they require a lot more work. My hesitation made her nervous and she retracted.

"It's not that I don't want to. I would actually love that. It would give me someone to work with, bounce ideas off of and especially after doing this wedding I'm realizing that it's difficult to pull off a job any bigger than this on my own." I paused not sure if I should continue but I saw no harm in telling her the truth. "Hannah, it's just that my husband, Nicholas, well he's the one that encouraged me to do this in the first place but now it is taking up so much of my time and he feels like I need to be home with Abby more. So, I'm just not sure if he would go for me expanding my business. I think his preference would be that I quit all together."

"Is that what you want?"

"No." I said it almost too quickly, surprising myself.

"Well, hmmm. I know what you mean. My husband isn't big on me going out a lot either but maybe there is a solution here."

"What do you mean?"

"Well, what if we did one job every couple of months together, at the most. Then, any little jobs that came up we could split. Like, I would take one, then you would take one. Like that."

"Hmm, that just might work. I'd have to see some of your work though. Maybe you could make a few samples for me or something?"

"Of course! I wouldn't expect anything unless you thought I could bring something to the table – no pun intended!" I couldn't help but laugh. It was nice to be around someone with a sense of humor. Then I thought how strange it was to laugh and how I missed it.

"Well, let me talk to Nicholas about it and see what he thinks."

"Sounds good, just call me sometime in the next couple weeks." We exchanged phone numbers and said our goodbyes. I had a good feeling about her but I didn't have a good feeling about what Nicholas would say.

58 - Megan

I sat on my back patio enjoying my flowers, the Arizona sunshine and a sweet breeze, one of my favorite things about this state. The air here always has softness to it that makes me feel like I have a cushion around me as I move through my day. I often sit out here on my day off while Jeff is at work, reading or just soaking up the serenity. I heard a distinct ring in the background and I opened my eyes and looked down at my cell phone on the table next to me. It was Becca. Believe it or not I haven't talked to her in about a week. This is rare for us since she usually calls me at least every other day. If I don't hear from her for 4 or 5 days, I usually call to make sure things are okay because if that much time goes by without a word from her, it usually means something is going on that she knows I wouldn't approve of.

"Hey Becca, I was beginning to wonder if you had dropped off the face of the earth!" I joked.

"I know it's been a while. How have you been?"

"Oh, I'm great. I have the day off today and I'm just kickin' back on my back patio in the Arizona sunshine."

"I'd call you a name but it wouldn't be nice." We laughed, it was always the joke of the conversation – how good the weather was here and how everyone else suffered the rain, hail, and freezing temperatures. We had our share of extremes though. The summers become insufferable by the time September rolls around and you are so sick of seeing triple digits on the news that you don't even watch anymore. Also, there can be monsoons in the summer, but as residents, we usually look forward to those because it's a change in the monotony of *beautiful and sunny*.

"Yeah, yeah. I bet it's nice there though."

"It is, it's about 82 today so I can't complain either."

"So, I'm sure you didn't call to talk about the weather. How are things going?" I just remembered she catered a wedding recently, "how did that wedding go? I want to hear all about it!"

"Oh, Megan, it was just beautiful and everyone loved the cake and the hors d'oeuvres! It couldn't have been better."

"Oh, that's such great news. I knew you would do great – you were born to do this!"

"Well, there's a little problem. I wanted to get your opinion."

"Okay." I sensed a hesitant disappointment in her voice.

"Nicholas and I were talking the other night and to make a long story short he feels like the catering is taking away from raising Abby and time we spend together. He thinks I should take it down a notch." I could just imagine how *that* conversation went. *You will quit catering!* I could just hear it.

"Wow, well what do you think?" I did my best, when I could control myself, to let her come to her own conclusions because it was her life and I could tell her what to do all I wanted but until she felt like it was what she wanted, she would never follow through and stand up for herself.

"I don't know. That's why I called my genius friend Megan! I've been torn over the whole thing. I love catering and it's really given me a sense of pride in my life, you know?"

"I can imagine! A woman's got to have something to call her own for God's sake. Plus, it must feel good for people to love your food and give you a sense of being appreciated, which I would imagine you don't get much from anywhere else." She went silent for a moment. Oops, I had to open my big mouth.

"Here's where it gets tricky. In order to get him off my back about it, I told him that this wedding would be my last job, but a friend of Tracy's, her name is Hannah, came up to me at the wedding. We got to talking and she mentioned maybe going into business together. I told her I would think about it and talk to Nicholas but I don't know if I should even bring it up."

"Hmm, good question. You don't want him to freak out."

"Preferably not."

"How would you and Hannah split up the work?"

"Well, we would do large events together – I discovered it's a lot of work to do a wedding on my own, thank goodness it was a small one! Then, the small jobs we would rotate and only accept one a month. She works too so she doesn't want it to be a full-time job or anything. It's a hobby for both of us so I thought that might work out. What are your thoughts?"

This was a tough one. I wanted to tell her *screw him, follow your dream* but I was well aware of the consequences that could be paid for challenging something he felt passionately about. He has never been a fan of her being out of the house much unless it benefits him somehow so I'm sure he has strong feelings about this.

"Maybe you could approach it gingerly and compromise with him somehow. You could start with telling him how you would be home much more often than before but still be able to cater once in a while if you had Hannah help you out. He gets what he wants and you get what you want."

"Yeah, maybe he would go for it if I put it that way."

"I have to say though Becca, be careful okay. I'm sure nothing crazy will happen and I hate that you would even have to consider this, but if you get the feeling it will push him over the edge then drop it."

"He'll be fine I'm sure. He's probably just worried about Abby, plus I have been gone a lot so he just misses me. I really should be flattered. I thought about dropping the catering all together just because – well I should probably be putting my family first."

Is she really going to let herself get brainwashed again? He doesn't miss her – although that would be nice if it were true – he just wants to know where she is, to have more control. "Becca, he's reverting to his old self again, it was bound to happen. Let's see, how long has it been? Just over a year? That's about right. A little over a year and he's starting to get comfortable again so he's letting his true colors shine through."

"I don't think so Megan, you don't see him every day. He's different than he used to be. He helps out with dishes and takes care of Abby. He actually *cares* this time."

"We'll see." I had serious doubts about that. It didn't take much to put your best foot forward for a year. That's pretty much what dating is.

"You know what, I'm sick of people not having a little faith in my decisions. It's *my* life and I'm the one that sees him every day. I've been through this before Megan! Don't you think I would know if he was lying to me? Give me a little credit! God forbid he cares about me and Abby! God forbid he actually changed so that he could have his family back! Is that so impossible? Everyone has bad days and everyone has things they feel strongly about. He can't have that like everyone else?"

Whoa! Now that's the side I wish she would show *him* once in a while. I must have crossed a line. I felt bad about making her go on the defensive and realized that I should at least give her the *impression* that I am giving him the benefit of the doubt.

"Becca, I'm sorry. Of course, he cares about you and Abby. I just got carried away. Anyone can change if they really want to, right?"

"Yeah."

"Hey, let me know how it goes okay? I'm sure once you explain the catering situation to him, he'll understand that it will be the best compromise."

"I think so too. Well, I gotta go, Abby is up and she's probably going to be hungry."

"Okay, well tell her hello from her Auntie Megan! I really have to get out there again so I can see her."

"I know. That would be great!"

"Okay, I'll talk to you later."

"Bye."

59 - Rebecca

"Eat your mac and cheese!" I teased, "Mommy has to do bills."

"Billths."

"That's right, peanut. Yucky bills!" I tickled her and she giggled.

"Yucky!" She mimicked me and I laughed.

The past two weeks have been blissfully normal. Nicholas and I had a good conversation about my catering business and he seemed to think it was a good idea. Megan had made me a little nervous about his reaction but it turned out I had nothing to be nervous about. He reassured me that he wanted me to be happy but he missed having me home more. I contacted Hannah and we had everything set up in case we were asked to do another job. I had to admit she was good, especially her peanut butter crackles.

Ugh, I hate doing bills and yet here I am sitting at the table in front of our laptop surrounded by a mound of paper. I still had residual receipts from supplies I had purchased and was realizing that it took a big chunk out of our monthly funds. Good thing I would be sharing in the cost of any future supplies! I noticed the balance of our account was only 31 dollars and 17 cents; how is that possible? Nicholas just got paid last week and I haven't spent money on anything since then except for the phone bill.

Just then, it occurred to me that we could be a victim of – what is that called – identity theft. Oh God! Now we'd have to change our accounts, all our credit cards, everything! Just the thought of it exhausted me. I started looking at each transaction over the past couple of months and matching it up with the check register. I noticed random large cash withdraws from the ATM up the street and a couple in various suburbs of Denver. I also noticed two debits from the casino for amounts over 300 dollars each! Where was he spending the rest of the money?

We still had to pay rent, utilities, and the car payment and we didn't have it. The only good thing was that with the grace period we could still make the rent payment on time using his next check.

All the money that I had deposited from the wedding I catered was gone. This was hard for me to come to terms with. I always thought that regardless of who brought home the money, it was for *us* but that meant that we both knew where it was going, that was only fair right? If he was just blowing money on the casino, I would find it hard not to be furious. He must have an explanation. Why would he spend money like that knowing that it would put us in a situation where we wouldn't be able to pay our bills? The door opened and I jumped in surprise.

"Hey babe. Abby, how's my little girl? Enjoying your mac and cheese I can see." She was covered in cheese. She had noodles in her hair and cheese all over her face and ears. I hadn't noticed before and I couldn't help but laugh.

I stood up to clean her off. "How was work?"

"Not bad, busy. You know the drill." He walked to the refrigerator and held it open scanning it for beer. We had one left at the very back on the middle shelf.

"Damn, only one left? You didn't go to the store today?" This would be the perfect time for me to mention the fact that we had *no* money.

"Well, actually I was just doing bills and there's only thirty dollars in our account."

"Oh my God! Are you really going to do this to me right now?" He raised his voice in frustration. I wet a washcloth and began wiping Abby down.

"Nicholas, we still have to pay rent, the car payment and util -," he interrupted me.

"No shit Becca! You don't think I know that? I'll take care of it, don't worry about it. I work my ass off! All I want to do is come home and relax and I get the third degree!"

I jumped at his response and was shaking inside but I had to know what his reasoning was. My frustration was valid and it wasn't my fault! I wasn't going to let him twist it into being *my* problem when it was his. "Where did the money go Nicholas? I'm sure you have a good reason. Just clue me in okay?" I tried to calm him down.

He took a swig of beer and slammed it down on the counter, "It's none of your God damn business!"

Abby started crying and screaming, her little face looking around the kitchen for something stable to hold on to. I unhinged her high chair and took her in my arms giving Nicholas a look; *look what you did.* I shushed her telling her everything was going to be okay and walked her upstairs. I would not subject her to this conversation and the only thing I could do was to put her to bed early. Unfortunately, I knew that would ruin the rest of my night since she would be up about the time, I wanted to go to bed but you do what you have to do, I guess.

I walked down the stairs after about ten minutes of calming Abby down and whispered firmly to Nicholas, "What the hell is your problem?"

"Oh, so it's *my* fault?"

"Yeah! You're the one that had to yell. You're the one that is spending hundreds of dollars of *our* money on who knows what and because of that we can't pay bills!"

"It's *my* fuckin' money sweetheart, not yours!" He spoke harshly in a voice that was so patronizing it made me feel five years old. "I'll spend *my* money wherever the hell I want to. If I want to go to the casino to get away from my wife because she's being a bitch then I will!"

I just stood there stunned. My entire body felt like ice and flames all at the same time. What happened to him? He hasn't called me that in years and he knows how much I hate the use of that word in general. My mind was stuttering trying to think of something to say that would erase everything but nothing was coming to me. I was in such shock that tears would not even fall from my eyes.

"What? Now you got nothin' to say? What happened, you lose your nerve?" He was being so cruel, like a bully on a playground taunting and patronizing me until I had nothing left of myself.

I looked down aching to prove him wrong; that I didn't lose my nerve, that I wasn't thrown off by his insanity, "How are we going to pay the car and utilities?" I tried to focus on the details hoping for a reprieve.

He rushed at me, grabbing both my arms and pinned me up against the wall. "You never listen! I said I'd take care of it didn't I?" He pounded his fist against the wall right next to my face and I flinched and turned my head, cowering lower against the wall.

All of the sudden, I was sitting on the floor and his hands were cradled around my face. I opened my eyes and met his.

"Becca, I'm sorry. I didn't mean to scare you. You just push me so far you know?" No words came to me. My ability to speak faded and all language melted off my tongue. I felt a rush of pain in my head and hot tears of sweet release fall on my cheeks. I shook my head in rejection of his apology and tried to stand but he wouldn't let me.

"Everything's going to be okay. We have plenty of money, the bills will be paid, don't worry about it okay? Besides, the world won't end if we're a little late this month, we have each other, right? I love you so much."

Did we have each other? I wasn't sure who was in front of me saying these words to me right now because it sure as hell wasn't my husband. This wasn't Nicholas. I felt like I was falling into an abyss and screaming for help but he just stood over me laughing. His demeaning words echoed in my ears and I had to escape. All I knew was that I didn't want the man responsible for breaking me apart to put me back together anymore.

60 - Nicholas

She stormed up the stairs crying and slammed the door for my benefit. I grabbed the car keys and headed for the door then stopped just as my shaky fingers grabbed the handle. *Shit.* I threw the keys somewhere off to my left and sat down in my favorite chair with my head in my hands. As I stared at the stained carpet below, my eyes began to fill and my throat felt on the brink of exploding if I held back any longer. Moments in time flooded my memory and I let go.

I saw Becca's face as I walked in the door, potholders on her hands and a smile on her face, us giggling on the kitchen floor, tubing down the river when we were just kids – it seemed like ions ago. I saw her dancing with Abby trying to get her to go to sleep and her coming home exhausted after working a 15-hour day while I was in school. I heard her voice in my head saying *I love you, I'm fine, don't worry about it, we'll get through.*

Then I saw myself through her eyes and felt ashamed of who I had become, who I had been. I was not the man I had planned to be, not even close, and I'm sure I was not the man she needed me to be. How did all this happen? How did we get here? I went from the knight on a white horse to the self-centered husband and half-ass father. Every argument we have I push her more and more until she breaks. Sometimes I even know I'm doing it, but at the time I don't give a shit and I'm not sure why. Sometimes the look on her face is one of hope and doubt all twisted into a red knot of tears pleading me to stop, but it's too late. I've chosen the words that I know cut the deepest and before I know it, she's almost gone. It is then and only then that I might retract my anger and tell her I love her, that I can't live without her. It's only in this vulnerable moment when I think I might lose her that I tell her how I truly feel.

She deserves better; I know that. I just don't know how to give her what she needs. I pleaded with her out loud in a desperate whisper. *Please just hang on baby. I'm about to come alive - for you, for Abby. Please wait for me; I can do it. I know I can.* God knows she is long overdue for something good to come her way and I wish I could be that something for her. I will be. I lifted my head and wiped my eyes ready to start over. I walked to the table in earnest and rifled through drawers until I found paper and a pen. If I couldn't tell her in person, I would write it down and then maybe she would understand. Maybe then she could really hear what I had to say.

    Becca,

       Don't give up on me. I love you and I can't do this without you. Please give me a chance to make it right. I promise I'll do better.

61 - Rebecca

I woke up bitter and empty but still trying to justify what happened last night in the far corners of my mind. It was still early and Abby would be asleep for at least another 45 minutes if I were lucky, so I decided to go downstairs and relax with some tea before the routine of the day began. I put the water on the stove and noticed a piece of paper on the table with writing on it. I squinted at it, my eyes still tired from lack of sleep. It didn't look like a bill so I walked over and sat down at the table. Nicholas had written me a letter? It's been years since he's written so much as a note to me. I read it over and over again trying to hear his voice speaking the words and trying to picture his face, as he would say it to me.

It was a letter pleading for me to give him a chance. Could he be worried that I might leave him? Honestly, I hadn't thought of it until now but it felt good that he was worried about us and that he didn't *want* me to leave. I was stripped of my daydreams by a high-pitched whistling. The tea! I ran over and turned off the burner, hoping that the shrieking didn't wake Abby. There was something about the feeling of hot tea flowing through my body in the morning, relaxing each muscle, smoothing over each thought, and easing my mind about the hours and days ahead.

He made a mistake, he was angry. I repeated this to myself over and over as I sipped my tea and stared out the window at the green grass and flickering leaves. *It's not who he is.* His words returned to me *you just push me so far.* Maybe I did push him too hard. If I didn't push so much, he probably wouldn't have flown off the handle. He's been amazing for so long and he has been so understanding about the new catering arrangements. I just couldn't believe for a minute that he was reverting to his old self like Megan said. I thought about the money and the transactions I had seen online in our checking account. *Why wouldn't he tell me where he spent the money?* I stood up to add more hot water to my tea. I guess it could be a guy thing. Maybe he felt like I was trying to get every little detail. I hated to be the 'nagging wife' but if it were no big deal why wouldn't he just tell me?

The money was something I just couldn't wrap my mind around but I figured that he would tell me in time, when he didn't feel so pressured and as long as we had money to pay bills, why should I complain? If there is one thing in a marriage that causes problems, besides money, it's miscommunication. It can make or break everything and I had to chalk last night up to just that – miscommunication. What we *really* needed was some time to ourselves to get back on track. We needed time to be us so that we could reconnect and with Abby needing our attention it was a little more difficult.

I smiled at my epiphany and felt a new flood of energy and positivity take over. I was ready to start over – rekindle the fire! I dialed my favorite babysitter, Jen, to see if she could watch Abby this evening for a few hours so that Nicholas and I could have dinner.

Since we didn't have a lot of money, I decided to cook one of his favorite meals. I have to admit, it's been a long time since I cooked a full meal from scratch for the two of us and I just know he would appreciate it.

At the sound of his truck pulling into the driveway, my heart skipped in my chest and I rushed around the kitchen putting the last of the dishes on the table and lighting the two candles. I had also primped a little – okay a lot. I had on a black dress that was a little shorter than I would have liked, but something Nicholas would enjoy, and one that I would never wear in public because it showed way too much of my legs, which now have stretchmarks. I have had to relearn my body since Abby was born. Everything feels different and clothes don't look the same but after trying on three different outfits, I resolved that I couldn't do anything tonight to change my body, I just had to work with what I had. I curled my hair and applied makeup so that my eyes looked dark and mysterious and my lips were glossy and sexy in a natural pink color called peach schnapps. I looked in the mirror for the last time, *damn girl, you clean up good!*

Not only did I want to see Nicholas melt at the sight of me, but also, I wanted to feel myself melt in his arms again. The cold words and defensive stares had become a barrier between us lately and I couldn't get myself to enjoy being close to him again. Instead of feeling lost in the sensation of his fingers on my skin I would tense against his shape and find myself thinking of what I thought he was hiding, words he had or hadn't said and other random things about catering, like what types of cakes or snack I hadn't yet discovered.

I leaned against a kitchen chair with as much finesse as I could muster, waiting for him to open the door. My hands were sweaty and my legs weak in anticipation and without the chair, I was sure I would fall over. The door finally squeaked open and the first thing I saw were the heads of beautiful red roses. I caught my breath at the thought of us finally being on the same page. He must have changed at work because he was wearing slacks and a black button-down shirt. He looked up as he was about to head down the hall and as soon as he saw me, he stopped in his tracks and literally almost dropped the flowers. *Just what I was looking for.*

I lifted my arms and twirled slowly, "Surprise."

He stepped forward and held out the flowers to me, "Surprise."

We embraced desperately, tears falling from both our eyes in a release of all the words neither of us had the courage to say. It was in that moment that we didn't need any words. We understood each other's gesture of surrender. We stood back from each other and wiped our eyes and we laughed at ourselves.

"You look – stunning!"

"Thank you," I walked over to the sink to put the flowers in some water admiring their sweet scent. "You look amazing yourself! It's so crazy how we both kind of had the same idea."

"I guess we're just that good." I smiled at him.

"Are you hungry?"

"Do you even have to ask? Becca, it looks absolutely delicious! We haven't done this in a *long* time."

"I know. That's why I thought it would be nice." We sat at the table both feeling like we were on our first date minus the mystery.

"Oh, where's Abby? Is she asleep?"

"Jen is watching her. We pick her up at eight." I winked at him and he smiled back.

"You're a genius."

"Well, I try."

We talked and laughed through dinner without one awkward quiet moment. We began to get to know each other all over again. He was funny, interesting and a flirt, tugging at my heart and drawing me in closer with each look. He hung on my every word and I had forgotten what it felt like for someone to truly listen to me. He seemed intrigued by each story I told and it made me feel valued and adored. Following dinner, we had dessert on the living room floor with the lights turned down low and music swaying in the background.

We danced in our bare feet and soon dissolved into each other so that I could no longer tell where I ended and he began. He kissed every inch of my trembling body and I watched him as if I had never seen him before, his hands melting around me like butter. I allowed myself to drown in his caress and gave myself over to him completely without holding back. I lay there next to him, on the living room floor, naked and exposed but feeling for the first time in years, completely safe. There was a soft comfortable weight to the air around me and all I could do was look at this man next to me and smile at my fortune. We were an *us* again.

Eventually we had to give in to the hands of time and end our glorious evening. We changed, had a few more bites of what was left of the pie and reluctantly drove to Jen's house to pick up Abby.

I looked over at my husband and he met my eyes, "I love you."

"I love you too, forever." My body quivered, giddy with emotion.

We sat in the dark, holding hands in silence as he drove. A question rose to the forefront of my thoughts and I pushed it away just as quickly, refusing to doubt this newfound connection. *How long will this last?*

62 - Eveline

"Kerner!"

"Right here." I waved my arm and took the mail eagerly as we all did. Any contact from anyone on the outside was welcomed. This week was a treat for me because only a few days ago I had received a letter from Rebecca with a picture of her and Abby enclosed. God, she was adorable. Abby looked just like Rebecca except for the eyes and from the sound of the letter she had her personality too. It was a good letter, Rebecca sounded like her and Nicholas were getting along and that they had found a way to reconnect and be a couple again.

I know Rebecca has always craved that sense of family ever since her dad and I were divorced. She seemed to always be missing that. I knew she would do anything to keep that dream alive and it sounded like she had. There is nothing like watching your kids grow up, especially when you get a chance to see them make choices in life that make them happy. When she is hurt, I feel her pain, when she rejoices in love and happiness, my heart wants to explode for her. I have been praying every morning and every night that she finds what she is looking for and that somehow her and Nicholas can understand each other and be happy together so that Abby can grow up with loving parents.

Neil and I almost made it. Rebecca was 16 or so when we divorced and although we didn't do it on purpose, it turns out that the teenage years are one of the worst times to drag a child through a divorce. It just kind of happened that way. It was like twirling as a child. You spin and spin and spin until you lose all sense of direction and all balance and control until you finally fall to the ground, only to find yourself still spinning. Nothing made me feel more complete than to know Rebecca was finding happiness in her life through her marriage and her newfound love of catering. I *never* liked cooking so I'm not sure where she gets it. Cooking always took so much time away from everything else I thought was important at the time and I was simply not patient enough.

Patience is a quality that I have learned to develop in prison. I have had no choice.

I have been eager these past few months to receive news regarding my mother's will. James was supposed to provide me with the details once everything was finalized. I didn't dare look to see whom the letter was from until I reached my cell. *James! Thank God!* I read the letter with such deliberate speed and precision that when I was finished, I realized my face was only six inches from the page. I laughed at my eagerness and sat back against the cold cement wall and smiled in relief.

The money will not go to Rebecca but be kept in a separate account, at Dad's request, for me to inherit when I am released from prison. Each brother was given an account with his respective inheritance from her mother. James would have access to my account because he was the executor of the will. He stated that he would be happy to help me if I needed something. As the victim's husband, my father inherits Mother's estate and then it will be his decision as to what happens with the money. I know that my father will help me. He always understood me better than my mother, even as a child. He has even told me now, that he understands me and knows that I would never have done anything intentionally to hurt her or anyone. It is my father that has always believed in me and I know he won't let me down. The stress of how I would manage after being released from prison was temporarily lifted. Daily, I would wonder where I would stay, where I could work, how would I travel, how can I start over? Now, that heavy weight has been lifted from my shoulders by God, he has answered my prayers. I will be safe now, no matter what happens.

63 - Rebecca

"You look amazing! I mean it, you should buy more shirts like that." Jen was the fashion guru and convinced me to go shopping with her – just us, no kids. Nicholas didn't really want me to go but he resigned himself to it and was taking Abby to the park while I was out gallivanting. It was more fun than I had remembered. For the longest time I haven't had the time or money to go shopping and I guess when you don't do something for so long you become more satisfied living without it. I was having a blast though!

"You think so? You don't think it's too bright?"

"No, you're getting it." My phone rang for the third time since we left the house.

"Oh, hold on." I shut the dressing room door and began to change back into my clothes while talking on the phone.

"Nicholas, hey what's up?"

"Nothing, just wanted to see what you were doing."

"Well, we're still shopping. Pretty much the same story as a half hour ago."

"Oh, cool. What store are you at?"

I had to think for a second since we had been in so many different stores. "We're in J Crew. I think I might have found a couple of cute things." I could hear Jen sigh quietly outside the dressing room.

"Aren't they kind of an expensive store?"

"Don't worry, I'm looking at the clearance rack."

"Well, whatever."

"Alright, Nicholas I really have to go Jen's waiting for me."

"Where you going next?"

I rolled my eyes, what is this, the Spanish Inquisition? "I don't know maybe another store, maybe get something to eat. I gotta go. Give Abby a kiss for me."

"Okay, bye."

I walked out of the dressing room with the shirt over my arm. I looked at Jen and rolled my eyes in reference to the phone call. "Sorry about that."

"He just can't live without you huh?"

"I guess not." We checked out then decided to go get some pretzels and something to drink.

"So, what's the deal with him always calling you? I mean, how are you guys doing?" I had shared only minor details of arguments Nicholas and I have had but I wanted her to know that I was just as normal as her.

"Oh, I don't know. I'm irresistible I guess!" I joked posing as if I was a model.

"Well, that's true." She gave me a wink.

"How's Joel doing?" Her son had recently come down with the flu, which throws your entire world as a mother into chaos.

"Oh, he's *so* much better. I'm so glad that's over with. I was lucky enough to avoid it but Josh came down with it last week and he was worse that Joel!"

"I know what you mean. Men are the biggest babies when it comes to being sick."

"So true. I didn't mind though, in a way. It was nice to have him home and to take care of him. It's that motherly instinct. I couldn't have done it a day longer though!"

"Yes, enough is enough."

"Hey, do you mind if we stop at Macy's really quick before we head out? I saw an advertisement on TV that they were having a baby sale."

"How could they do that? How dare they sell babies!" We both laughed at my corny joke and just as we started to collect our things, my phone rang.

Jen looked at me, "Wow Becca, the man needs help."

"I know – hello?"

"Hey, Abby wanted to say hi."

"Well, tell her I said hi and that I'll be home soon."

"Are you on your way home now?"

"Well, not quite. We're going to stop at Macy's then probably head back. Do you think you can make it that long without me?" Jen laughed in the background.

"I guess I'll find out. Miss you."

"Miss you too, bye!" I hung up the phone regurgitating the conversation back to Jen knowing she would get a kick out of it.

Jen dropped me off at my house, "Well, I feel like I went out with you *and* Nicholas!"

"I know, I'm sorry about that."

She waved her hand in dismissal. "Don't lose sleep over it. It's actually kind of sweet. I swear sometimes Josh forgets that I'm even gone. I'll probably get home and he'll say *oh did you go out?*" We both laughed and said our goodbyes.

"Thanks!" I waved to her as she drove off and thought to myself how lucky I was to have a husband that at least cared about where I was.

The moment I walked in the door, Nicholas wrapped his arms around me. I was so taken aback by this that I dropped my shopping bags. "Wow, that's something new."

"I missed you. How was shopping?"

"It was good, want to see what I got?"

"Only if it's lingerie."

"Ha, ha. Check it out." I emptied my bags and held up each piece to him and Abby getting their approval. I felt admired. After my own personal fashion show, with Abby at the table having a snack, Nicholas looked over at me and smiled.

"What?" The attention was almost making me uncomfortable. It was probably because I just wasn't used to being missed.

"I don't know. I just feel neglected, we haven't really talked much today." Since when did he want to talk? I'm gone *one* day shopping and he feels neglected? A part of me wanted to say *suck it up, do you know how many days and nights I have had to be alone?*

"I'm sorry." He smiled, pulled me close and brushed the hair out of my face.

173

"Don't let it happen again." He laughed and kissed me so softly that I forgot about every other emotion swirling around in my head.

64 - Megan

I don't cook often; I guess that's why I still enjoy it. I stirred the spaghetti sauce and monitored the pasta as I listened to Becca's reading of a letter she had received from her mother. I thought back to the day that Becca had told me what happened. At first, I couldn't believe that a person like Eveline was capable of hurting another person in such a violent way, especially her own mother. I thought of all the times she had taken us out for ice cream or played dress-up with us or took us shopping. None of it made sense to me until I allowed myself to think of her as a woman instead of mother. It's funny how that changes things. It was only when I entered my mid-twenties that I began to think of my parents as people. They became men and women dealing with the same things I was but with even more baggage.

I knew of Eveline's history with her family and how she struggled in relationships. It didn't mean much to me until August 12th. At that time and for many months after, I wasn't sure how Becca could move on and still see her as a mother, still love her, still need her. Despite the horrific events of that day, no one including myself has the right to judge Eveline. I will never know the torment and regret she might experience or how it feels to be kept from your only daughter. Who is to say that in the right moment, given all the right ingredients, I wouldn't be pushed so far as to act violently against another person? Who is to say that Becca wouldn't defend her child so fiercely as to hurt another human being? I don't agree with violence, I never have. As a nurse I see enough of it in every form you can imagine and I am usually the one intercepting frustrations and attempting to heal people.

It is odd how time can diminish even an act as horrible as murder. It's been years since the day Eveline was sent to prison and listening to her letter to Becca, it was as if it had all disappeared. She had a new agenda and a new purpose and the reason she was there seemed to have vanished. I wondered what it was like for her brothers and her father. Did time take away their

175

pain as well or did it always remain just under the surface for both Eveline and her family? To survive each day did they have to mask their pain and press on as if nothing could hold them back? Despite the positive tone to the letter, I felt a deep sadness for her and Becca and I wasn't quite sure why.

"Megan?"

"What?"

"What do you think?"

"Well, I'm shocked to say the least. I was really counting on you being a millionaire!" I joked, trying to lighten her spirits.

She laughed, "Yeah, I knew that was never going to happen. Although I can't say Nicholas wasn't hoping for it!"

"No, in all seriousness I *am* surprised that she is allowed to inherit the money even if it *is* indirectly."

"I know, I was surprised too but I'm actually glad for her."

I stopped stirring and turned off the burner under the pasta, "You are?"

"Well, Megan she has close to nothing and when she gets out, she's never going to be able to find a job making the kind of money she was making before she went to prison. At least it will give her peace of mind and maybe a chance to have somewhat of a normal life when she gets out."

"Yeah, I guess I hadn't thought of it that way. It's true, she has no retirement to speak of – or at least not enough and no way of accumulating it through a job again."

"So, I'm happy for her."

"You are such a selfless person Becca. Sometimes I wish I could be more like that." I could hear the surprise in her voice.

"You want to be like me? That's a first."

"It's a good quality to have, you just take it a little far sometimes in other aspects of your life." I changed the subject before I got carried away about a subject neither of us could win at. "Are you going to visit her again anytime soon?"

"Yeah, maybe in the spring. I'm sure she would like it. I just have a lot going on right now so we'll wait and see."

"Hey! How is the catering business, you haven't mentioned it in a while?"

"It's slowed down a lot. Hannah and I meet once in a while to practice baking things here and there but not too much going on. We might have a wedding but I won't know for sure for a couple of weeks."

"Well, it's bound to slow down this time of year. Although a fall wedding *would* be pretty, just think of all the food you could make to go with a fall wedding!"

"I know! I'm crossing my fingers but trying not to be too hopeful."

"So, Nick is back on board and being supportive?"

She hesitated just for a moment, "Yeah, he's supportive. We had a talk about it a while ago and he liked that Hannah was splitting things with me, so it's been working out pretty good so far. He's been really great lately."

I didn't want her to go on a spree of justification and reasoning with me about why he was the five-star husband she always wanted so I just responded with a *good, that's great* and let the conversation die out. I had a feeling that she was holding something back. She seemed to be trying to convince herself more than she was trying to convince me and I was concerned for her. I have to admit that selfishly there was a part of me that just didn't want to know about what was really happening. I was so tired of her roller-coaster ride of a life that I wasn't sure I had the energy to go through it again. Just as this thought crossed my mind, I knew that I would never abandon her either. She was my best friend – like a sister to me and no matter how many times she needed me I would be there because I love her, no questions asked.

65 - Rebecca

I rolled over and searched with my hand finding the empty space beside me. Nicholas was at work, which meant Abby would be waking up soon. I smiled as the night's previous conversation crept back into my consciousness. Today would be a good day. After we put Abby to bed, we ended up on the couch talking for hours about everything; our own goals as well as what we wanted the future to hold for Abby. We shared funny stories about friends and family past times and laughed until our muscles ached. I haven't felt that way since we were dating.

As I was blow-drying my hair the day's chores suddenly came to me and I snapped back in to reality. I had to meet with Hannah, take Abby to get her shots, and clean the house, which I would save for last because it was the thing that I dreaded the most. Well, cleaning didn't bother me so much in general; it was cleaning the bathroom that I usually put off as long as possible. I don't know why, I guess because it took the most work. Now that Abby was getting a little older, I would enlist her to help with the little jobs like putting clothes in the hamper or sweeping the kitchen floor.

Hannah pushed past me in excitement as soon as I opened the door. "Becca, I have amazing news!"

"Don't tell me!"

"Yes!" We screamed and jumped up and down. "The Fuller wedding is all ours and we have five weeks."

"Oh, dear God, I think I might pass out." I felt a little dizzy and sat down next to Abby who was joining in our jubilation by screeching and clapping.

We spent the next few hours going over every detail of the wedding while Abby sat in her chair eating breakfast. This time we would be responsible for appetizers, entrées and the cake. We planned everything out on our calendars and pooled recipes in preparation. The bride and groom had already picked out a cake they wanted us to replicate and it would be a little tricky but doable. We were both looking forward to the challenge. We decided to split the appetizers and the entrées (they wanted the option of chicken or fish) but we would both work on the cake together. The cake was always the prize of the event and we both loved having a hand in it. It was the best part as far as Hannah and I were concerned.

"I can't wait!" I was looking forward to having a project again as well as working with Hannah. So far, we had each only done a couple of small events on our own. This would be the first job we would do together.

"I know, me too. Becca I just want to say thanks again for having faith in me and for letting me work with you. I've learned so much from you already and I can't wait to do this event together."

"Thanks. It's worked out great for me too." I gave Abby a new toy to play with since she was starting to get fussy.

"Well, I guess that's it."

"Okay, so I'll see you next week and we'll both hopefully have our appetizers and entrées set up by then and we can start working on the cake."

"Excellent."

"Alright, I'll see you then." I closed the door and looked down at Abby's mischievous smile.

"Guess what time it is?"

"No." She giggled and backed away from me playfully.

"Nap time!" I chased her around the house and up the stairs until she and I were both tired then finally got her to settle down for a nap. I walked to the end of the driveway to pick up the mail and put some leftovers in the microwave for lunch.

I sorted through the mail as I leaned with my back to the counter - credit card, credit card, power bill, a coupon to Lowe's, phone bill. I tossed everything but the bills and threw them on the table to look at while I was eating. I can't remember the last time I just sat and ate without doing something else at the same time. It's become a habit to multi-task, a talent developed even more after I had Abby.

"What? That can't be right." The phone bill was twice the amount it usually was. The last one had been slightly on the high side but not over 100 dollars higher. This was ridiculous and had to be a mistake. I only call Megan and a couple people locally but the minutes are free when I talk to Megan since we are in 'the network'. I took a bite of pasta salad and scanned the calls noticing a number that kept repeating. It looked somewhat familiar but not one that I knew very well. I grabbed the phone bill from last month and scanned it for the same number – yep, there it is. *Who is that?* I thought it might be a client from catering but it was repeating too often over too long a period of time to be anyone I've done work for.

I looked at the dates and times of the calls more carefully and tried to pick dates that I remembered doing something significant on. I went back to the beginning where I first saw the number appear. Why is *that* day familiar? I thought about the night I went out with Jen and Tracy, the night I saw Jack and pulled out the bank statement showing charges. Ah ha! Martini's Place, $10.71. It was the same day as the number on the phone bill and the call came in at 10:23 p.m. Then it hit me with all its weight, *Jenna*. I remember seeing her number when she sent him a text just after we got remarried.

My lunch was getting cold and hot tears were burning their way down my cheeks and blurring spots on the phone bill below. I frantically scanned the rest of the bill noticing that she called his cell phone about once a week around lunchtime, and a couple of times late at night when I would have been asleep. I thought back, there were many nights I would go to bed before him and he would say *I'm not tired yet, I'm just gonna watch a little TV, I'll be up in a bit.* My entire body was shaking and my neck was wet and sticky with my salty tears. I stared out at the back yard and let it blur in front of me. How could I be so foolish? How could I *not* see this happening right in front of me? Was everyone else right?

As I continued to punish myself with questions it occurred to me that it wasn't my fault, it was a decision he had made. All I had done since we were remarried is try to make him happy, to work at being an us and to compromise so that we could be happy together. *It's never enough.* He's the one that made the decision to talk to her and do God knows what else with her. I can't even think about that now, although deep down I knew the truth. I know he'll deny it till he's blue in the face but a woman knows when something isn't right. Maybe I knew a long time ago. Maybe I just chose to ignore the signs, wanting more than anything to think that this marriage was working. What else did I have?

I thought of the past month and how he *missed* me and how he *needed* me; it made me sick to think of the moments we had together that I interpreted as sweet but were all lies. Jenna was everything I wasn't and aside from the deceit, this struck a chord into the heart of my sense of self like nothing else could. They had probably shared moments of intense passion and mystery, her perfectly shaped body rising against his. It wasn't fair to me. They could share something that Nicholas and I could never again experience due to the fiery history that would always remain between us. If she only knew what he was like on the other side of the sheets, would she still want to ruin my life? Another surge of anguish shot through my body and I came to my knees on the dirty linoleum floor, crumbs sticking to my sweaty palms. *What do I do?*

"Mommy?" Abby. I cried even more upon hearing her voice. I hated that she saw me like this. I wiped my eyes trying to compose myself.

"Mommy, you okay? Why cwying?" She was the best thing that ever happened to me. I took her in my arms and held her.

"Mommy's okay sweetie, I'm just sad, that's all. Nothing to worry about." We sat there on the kitchen floor and I realized that it was *her* I should have been fighting for, not Nicholas. It was Abby that deserved better, not me. It was Abby who needed me, not Nicholas. How could I have been so selfish? More importantly, what would I do about it?

I pushed my sadness and anger aside and did what I could to move on with the day – for Abby's sake. We played at the park, took her to the doctor for her shots and stopped at the store. In my guilt, I succumbed to Abby's requests for candy and a toy horse she grabbed off the shelf.

I had prepared a simple dinner and was holding it on the stove when the phone rang. Wonderful, probably Nicholas. I took a deep breath in. *Pull yourself together, wait to have the conversation at home, be strong.*

"Hey Bec!"

I tried to sound as cheerful as I could, "Hey, how was work?"

"Great, hey I'm gonna stop by Ray's and have a couple of drinks with the guys but I won't be long. Is that cool?"

"Well, I had dinner all ready but I guess it doesn't matter." I couldn't hide my disappointment.

"What's your problem? We've been spending a lot of time together lately and I can't go out for a couple hours *one* night?"

"It's fine Nicholas, do whatever you want okay. Abby and I will eat and I'll just put the leftovers in the fridge." I felt nauseous just hearing myself talk to him. *Don't worry about it honey, I'll just be the one to constantly give in. You go have fun!*

"Yeah, whatever. I'll see you at home."

I didn't even say goodbye because I know I would have burst into tears. I hung up the phone and looked over at Abby watching cartoons. "Abby, dinner's ready! It's just you and me kiddo."

Abby and I had the best time together playing with her toys and playing make believe. I let go and let myself pretend. A bath and a bedtime story later, I was at the table with a cup of tea staring at the phone bill once again. This time I calculated my next steps knowing that there would be a long road ahead. No matter what, I had to be confident enough in myself to follow through so that Abby and I could have a better, more stable life, one that we deserved even if it was just us. I left the bill on the table, each phone call and text from or to Jenna highlighted in bright yellow with Jenna's name circled at the top and a note to Nicholas underneath. *We need to talk.*

The minutes crept by as I lay in our dark bedroom trying to find sleep. Finally, I dreamt of floating down a Montana river with Nicholas, laughing and splashing each other without a care in the world. I remember feeling weightless until all of the sudden I was under water. I tried to open my eyes but I didn't see anything but blackness. I struggled to breathe, the water turbulent and swirling around me. I woke up gasping for air and came face to face with Nicholas. He had my t-shirt in his fist and was shaking me and yelling something at me. I tried to tell him to stop, to ask him what was happening but I was so confused and he just kept yelling and shaking me. Finally, my head cleared and I defended myself by thrashing my arms and legs trying to break free of his grasp.

He reeked of alcohol and his skin was wet with perspiration. I fell out of his grasp and onto the floor noticing the red numbers of the alarm clock that had fallen next to me; 2:00 A.M. His words were slurred but I heard Jenna's name and *how dare you* and a barrage of foul language hurled directly at me. He pulled me up against the wall with one hand around my throat, my legs were trying to find something, anything to support the weight of my body. He swayed leaning against me to stop himself from falling and put his free hand under my shirt. I began to scream at him and writhe against the wall telling him to stop. I heard Abby crying in the background and knew she would be standing in the doorway soon and it was at that moment I had to find more strength than I knew I had.

I kicked him hard between the legs and as he went down, I pushed him away from me. He cried out in pain but stayed on the ground unable to move. I waited against the wall in the dark, breathless, hoping the obvious abundance of alcohol would kick in soon and he would pass out. My eyes adjusted and I met the whites of Abby's eyes at the doorway. She was crying and the moonlight peeking through the blinds made her tears sparkle. I ran to her and took her in my arms. Just before I closed the door behind me, I heard his muffled voice against the carpet. "Bitch."

I spent the night curled up beside Abby telling her stories of beautiful fairy princesses and butterflies in faraway lands.

66 - Nicholas

I have a headache from hell. First things first, coffee. In a rush, pieces of what happened the night before flooded my mind. Stunned at first, I shook my head. I refuse to apologize for the way I feel. She was getting out of control, gone all the time doing God knows what. She was beginning to have this arrogance about her and becoming more and more opinionated every day, which was getting under my skin. Who the hell does she think she is? I heard Becca's tentative steps make their way down the stairs. Abby was in her arms, still sleepy from the night. Becca's face was lightly bruised and red from crying. I felt a pang of guilt and smiled at her in attempt to lift her spirits.

"How are my girls this morning?" I rubbed Abby's head and kissed her, "Good morning sunshine."

Becca held my eyes with piercing anger and fear. I pushed her back with my eyes and went back to my newspaper.

"You're done with this catering thing." She settled Abby into her chair with a yellow bib that said *Mommy's girl* on it.

"You can't do that! I'm just getting started and I'm *really* good, I have that wedding coming up." I could almost hear what she would say if she had the guts. *It's all I have that is mine. Bastard.*

"We can't afford it," I lied, "do you want to feed your child or pursue your career? Your choice?"

"I do the bills and we are just fine or at least we would be if you wouldn't gamble away all our money and sleep around with whores!"

I jumped up quickly; my chair fell over and bounced on the linoleum behind me. Abby started to whine and cry, distressed at the loud noise and tension in the air. I came face to face with Becca and she backed up to the counter unable to go any further. I didn't say a word, just smiled, kissed her and walked out the door.

67 - Eveline

The ceiling has eyes. I stare back in awe at its lack of judgment and wonder if I will ever be in a world where I can be happy again. I'm not sure if I have ever been truly happy. Looking back at my life from this vantage point I know I should have been. I had a husband who would have and did do everything for me; I regret now that I took advantage of him. I had a daughter who adored me and looked up to me, a love I never could have imagined receiving and a job that I *loved*. I was foolish to think that I could rebuild my life or that I would get a second chance. James had come to see me and taken away all the hope that he had once given me.

When I entered 'the House' I was delighted and surprised to see James waiting at a visitor's table. He smiled and waved me over. We spoke for hours about his kids, Rebecca, Dad and his job. I told him all the teaching and writing that I had been doing and how I have been able to help so many people.

He seemed proud of me.

"Evy," he said looking down at the table, "there's something I need to talk to you about."

I have learned over the past year that silence is often the best answer so I waited for him to speak and held my breath.

"It's about the inheritance. There is still a portion of it that is yours, but there have been a few changes." He looked at me for approval and I nodded for him to go on. "Dad is deteriorating and he has been deemed incompetent to make decisions due to his mental state. He is too confused now Evy."

"Who made that decision?"

"Well, a judge and a lot of people were involved."

"Who initiated it?" He looked at me with sadness and coldness in his eyes.

"Look Evy, I had to okay. You don't know what he's like. Someone had to make the decision and it wasn't easy. I made the decision as executor to deny you access to the funds. I will have control of how they are dispersed. There will be money set aside for you, but I feel that due to the circumstances in which the money was received, there should be specific things the money can be used for."

"I don't understand."

"Evy," he slid a pile of legal paperwork in front of me, "the money will be available to you for attaining psychiatric counseling or related services, but that's it. You're on your own for living expenses." I just sat there with my mouth open. How could he go back on our father's wishes and take my only chance for having a life away from me?

"How could you do this to me James?!" My body rushed with heat and tears streaked my face.

He stood up and grabbed his jacket, "No Evy, *you* did this."

68 - Rebecca

"I just have to stop at the bank," Hannah pulled into the bank and I ran to the ATM. After weeks of work on the dishes and cake, we were on our way to the Fuller wedding and I wasn't sure which one of us was more excited. Behind my exhilaration though was suspicion. Each day was a struggle as I planned my next move, learning what worked and what didn't as I went. Regardless, I was looking forward to a day of thinking about something else. I was tired.

I punched in my pin a second time as I looked back at Hannah telling her *just one more minute*. The ATM spit the card back out to me and the screen read *Access to account *****4593 has been denied. Please call 1-800-543-0971 for more information.* What the hell was going on? This was a new card. I rushed back to the car and explained what had happened to Hannah.

"Hey, don't worry about it. It's on me today okay?"

"I'll pay you back Hannah, I'm sorry. Can I use your phone to call the bank really quick?"

"Sure." She sped off toward the Fuller house, a beautiful mansion-sized house with a huge backyard where the wedding and reception would be held. I snapped the phone shut, not even thanking the customer service rep – which I always did. If you have ever worked in customer service you know how people should be treated.

"Damn him!"

"What's going on? Is everything okay?"

"No!" I was close to hyperventilating but the fact that Hannah was sitting next to me kept me in check. "Nicholas. He – he took my name off our account. I have *no* access to money. I can't believe this!"

"Why the hell would he do that?" She looked very confused and I wasn't about to fill her in on all the details so I just told her we have been fighting a lot lately.

"He sounds like a control freak, no offense."

"None taken – believe me." We rode the rest of the way in silence, neither of us knowing what to say.

The cake was the star of the show and throughout the reception we had people come up to us and applaud us on either an appetizer or the magnificent cake. It was made up of five cream and white tiers swirled like a spiral staircase with various shells, starfish, and sand dollars clinging to the sides. Instead of a cake topper the bride and groom's names appeared as if they were written in sand with a heart around it. The idea was brilliant and Hannah and I pretended we had been to the ocean as we were constructing our masterpiece. It felt so good to be appreciated and acknowledged by people of all ages. We felt like celebrities. Everywhere I went I was reminded of how not everyone would hurt or try to take advantage of me, people could be good. *So, feeling frightened and self-conscious isn't normal?* I began to relax as the last of the guests were served. Hannah and I lifted our glasses of sparkling cider and toasted to a beautiful event and the genius caterers that made it a success.

I began to scan the crowd, laughing at some of the couples trying to dance and children stealing bites of cake from their parents. Just then I saw a familiar face and my entire body turned to ice. I felt like I was in one of those dreams where you try with all your might to move but you can't. You try to run but instead you are moving in slow motion and only seem to move a few inches.

Without looking away I got Hannah's attention, "Hannah. He's here."

"Who's here? Someone you know?"

"Nicholas is here."

"What? Why would he be here? That's kinda scary right?"

"Only slightly," I tried to be positive, "maybe it's Abby. I should go see if everything is okay."

"Right, that's true. Maybe, I'll hold down the fort."

I made my way through the crowds nodding in acceptance to flattery regarding the cake. I stepped behind a large rhododendron,

"Nicholas, what are you *doing* here? Is Abby okay? Is everything okay?"

"What? I can't visit my wife?"

"Since when have you visited me at a catering job?"

He ignored me, "Since when did you start drinking?"

"It's sparkling cider. Why are you here?"

He scanned the crowd with a smile and spoke to me without making eye contact. "You are going to quit tonight Becca. Abby and I need you at home."

I looked around in search for backup *is it only me that thinks this is ridiculous*? But of course, no one could hear us – not that it would have made a difference. The last thing I wanted was a scene at an event that was just pulled off with sensational ease. I calculated my options and their various consequences all in a matter of five seconds.

"Nicholas, can we talk about this at home? I'm almost done here." I tugged at his sleeve trying to appeal to a side of him I wasn't sure existed anymore. Maybe it never existed in the first place.

He turned to me and held my hand, "You might as well tell Hannah tonight. Why lead her on any longer than necessary? Besides you wouldn't want to take away both jobs from her, would you?"

"What?"

"I'm just saying it would be a shame to see her get fired from the school for getting a little too aggressive with the kids."

"They'll never believe you."

"Just try me."

"Right, loud and clear. I don't quit and you get her fired, that's just great Nicholas!" I looked over at Hannah serving cake to the flower girl, "Fine, have it your way – again. I'll quit. Are you happy now?"

"I'm happy that you are choosing to put your family first. Abby will be so excited when I tell her." He turned to leave, "I'll see you at home."

I didn't watch him leave. I stood there staring at Hannah until she caught my eye and sensed something wasn't right. She made her way to me and didn't ask me any questions; just took me in her arms and let me cry.

"Men!" she said, "I swear sometimes they do it just for fun."

I pulled away from her, wiped my eyes and composed myself, "Hannah, I have to hand the business over to you. This is my last event." My voice was shaking and I couldn't erase the regret. I knew by the look on her face that she understood the position I was placed in.

"Becca, I can't do this without you."

"You'll be great, I just know it. It's your turn to train someone new."

"It's not fair."

"I know. Life isn't fair is it?"

"Come on, let's go clean up. At least we can enjoy the rest of the night, right?"

"Yeah, at least we have that."

69 - Megan

I've heard it all before but my heart still ached for her and especially for Abby who is an innocent victim in a grown-up world. Jeff sat across from me in the living room rolling his eyes *here we go again*. It's not that he doesn't care about Becca, it's that he doesn't understand how a woman can stay with a man that causes her that much pain. No, not only *stay* with him but to continue to go back for more. He wants her to be happy just as much as I do, but of course Becca and I have a history, a tie that binds us together. I understand her and she understands me. I've told her countless times that she deserves better and that she doesn't need him and I will tell her a thousand times more if I have to, because I wish someone would have done that for me. I was fortunate enough to have the self-confidence to leave and I had met Jeff shortly after my previous relationship, so I had the idea of something better pulling me in the opposite direction. Becca doesn't have that which makes it twice as hard. Not to mention the fact that her and Nicholas have been together for years and friends in high school before that. Talk about history!

No one likes to start over, but Becca and Nicholas are headed for a collision.

"I'm sorry I didn't tell you about it sooner Megan."

"Becca, you don't have to explain yourself. It's your life and you have the right to keep it to yourself if you want to. You know I'm here for you if you need me. I'm glad you're telling me now." I had to suppress the urge to scream. She needed to get out *now*! I didn't want to push her though, she had to make this decision on her own otherwise she would just end up back where she started, again.

"I know what I need to do, I just need you to tell me I can do it."

"Becca, if you don't leave soon you are putting yourself and Abby in danger. It sounds like Abby has already witnessed more than you would have liked. Not to mention Becca, she's getting older and understands more than you think she does. She might not be able to understand exactly what's going on but she can feel the tension. I see lots of kids at the hospital with internalized anger or tension because of stressfull home life situations."

Becca began to cry, "I know, I know. That hurts me the most." She was silent for a moment collecting herself, "Megan, you don't understand. It's not that easy. Everyone says *just leave* but there's so much more to it than that. I don't think I've ever been this scared."

"I don't blame you."

"Sometimes it's not even *him* that I'm scared of. I'm concerned that I won't have the courage to make it on my own. I worry that he'll convince me to stay."

"I know. Nothing worth doing is ever easy. I'll tell you what. Jeff and I have been talking and how would you feel if we flew out there?

"You guys are so sweet. I appreciate the offer Megan, but this is something I have to do on my own. I can handle it."

"Okay, well the offer is there if you change your mind."

"I just have to get going on the paperwork aspect of things, all the little details. This time I have to do it without him knowing though."

"Good idea. It doesn't sound like he would handle it all that well if you handed it to him yourself."

"I just need to bide my time for now." I knew what that meant. I could just picture Becca being a human doormat for that asshole. Just the thought of her cooking him dinner and cleaning up after him, doing what she was told, made my skin crawl. An uneasiness crept through my body for her.

"Alright, well keep me posted on how things are going and if you need *anything* you let me know. I mean it."

"Okay, I will. Oh, Megan?"

"Yeah?"

"Thanks for not saying I told you so."

"I would never do that. I love you."

"Love you too."

70 - Nicholas

I sat at my desk staring out the window at the city and tapping a pencil on the polished mahogany. I'd been at work for three hours and despite my best efforts, was unable to concentrate. I felt like I was losing Becca and I couldn't get her beautiful face out of my mind. I must have gone a little overboard the night she left the note about Jenna. I don't really remember much about that night but by the look on her face the next morning, I could tell it wasn't good. Jenna and I were just goofing around – it didn't mean anything.

I knew Becca wouldn't understand and I couldn't bear to tell her the truth so we both allowed it to slip through the cracks of our marriage preferring to let it disappear. She was my wife; the only woman I truly loved and I would do anything to make her stay. Lately she seemed like she was going through the motions of each day but was always somewhere else and it tore at my heart that she was so distant. I looked at my watch. 11:13 a.m. I had to see her.

"Jerry!" I walked next door to my boss's office. "I have to take off for a couple hours."

"What the hell for?"

"Something's come up with my daughter," I lied, "I'll be back after lunch." I didn't wait for his answer. I was his favorite employee ever since we clinched the Colorado Springs museum account and I could get away with murder. Maybe I would surprise Becca with some flowers and take her out to lunch. She was probably folding laundry at the house or something. I pictured her fluid movements and her surprise at my arrival for lunch. Becca couldn't resist flowers and I haven't taken her out to lunch in years.

I pulled into the house with daisies I had picked up at Rite Aid on the way home.

"Becca? Abby? Surprise!" No one answered. I searched each room downstairs, then upstairs. Where the hell is she? She never mentioned going anywhere today. The car was in the driveway.

Silence filled the house and felt heavy on my shoulders as I stood there feeling more and more foolish. I walked out, slamming the door behind me letting rage cover me like a warm blanket. *She can't be far.*

I drove by all the places I thought she could be and finally spotted her as I drove by a little café about a mile from the house. Could that be her? I pulled past the café and parked in the video store's parking lot across from it. She was sitting outside with Abby, Tracy, Jen and their kids. She looked so relaxed and happy. She was actually laughing! I searched my memory and couldn't picture a time in the last six months that I had seen her laugh. I know she was with her friends but I couldn't help but feel jealous. Why could she be this other person with them and not with me?

I hopped out of the truck, the daisies limp in my fist as I made my way across the pavement. Abby saw me before anyone else, "Daddy!"

Becca whipped around in her chair and her friends went quiet. "Nicholas. What are you doing here?"

"Well, I was bringing you these!" I shoved the flowers in her face, angry that she had made a fool of me and taken away my plans for a wonderful afternoon. "But *you* weren't home!"

"Well," she stuttered looking at her friends, "Tracy and Jen invited Abby and I to have lunch."

"You ruined everything. Let's go!" I pointed toward the truck and lifted Abby off the ground.

"Nicholas!"

Was she really going to push me? "I said, let's go!" I grabbed her arm and lifted her out of the chair, pulling her along side of me. She looked back at them and Abby began to cry. I pushed Becca into the truck and buckled Abby in.

"I'm disappointed in you Becca."

"I was just having lunch, how is that disappointing?"

"Don't be a smart ass. *We* are going to have lunch together. I won't let you ruin my plans and make me look like a complete idiot. I took off work to have lunch with you and Abby and that is what we are going to do." The mangled flowers lay in her lap and she stared silently out the window while Abby whimpered in the back seat.

71 - Eveline

My dearest daughter,

Nothing brings me more joy than to know you are happy. I'm glad things are going so well for you with Nicholas and your catering business. I know you will do well. You are a talented, beautiful girl and I'm so proud of you. There are some things that I need to tell you. Do you remember when your dad and I took you camping next to the Bitterroot River that summer? You were so excited at every little thing, the rocks, the flowers, cooking over a fire. Everything fascinated you and I never forgot that. You taught me that day to look at things that I had seen a thousand times with fresh eyes. When I looked at those things around me through your eyes, it was a world yet to be discovered. Those days were some of the happiest of my life. Your dad, you and I were in our own little world for a precious two days and I'll never forget it. I still think of those days at night when I can't sleep and it gives me peace.

When you visited last, you asked me about what happened the day the world fell around me, August 12th. I feel now, that I must tell you. I only hope that you can forgive me for all the pain I know I have caused you.

Like I said, Mom fell down the stairs and I reached out to stop her from falling but I didn't grab her in time. She was screaming and hurling insults at me like I was nine years old, telling me how she wished she never had me and how it was all my fault that her sons were dead. That's when I snapped, suddenly feeling removed from myself like I was watching it all happen. I remembered that I had put the hammer in the drawer when I was cleaning up before they arrived. I broke free from her grasp and ran to the kitchen finding the hammer and a garbage bag.

I know how difficult this must be for you to read. I have never put it into writing before, never mind allowing myself to remember the events as they actually happened that morning. I know you will understand why I am telling you the truth. You are the only one I have ever told. I have had a long full life, with more experiences, good and bad, than I could have dreamed of. I have made and lost friends and loved ones and, in the end, it is you, my only daughter that I lean on and trust. I never thought I was capable of loving someone so much until I had you. I'm so glad you were born.

Life is messy Rebecca. We are all colliding with each other in pursuit of our own agendas but I think we all really want the same thing – to matter to someone. Thank you for making me feel like I matter to you. I'll always love you.

Mom

72 - Rebecca

With Abby down for a nap and Nicholas at work I finally had a chance to think. I was finding it hard to focus but I knew what I had to do and that I had to concentrate on one short-term goal at a time otherwise I would never get through this. What kept me going was the thought that things could be better someday. I clung to the hope that I could make it up to Abby and give her what she needed to become a happy, well-adjusted woman who wouldn't seek out destructive men like I did. If I could prevent that one thing in her life, I had to take a chance, even if it meant risking my security.

I happened to see an advertisement the other day on TV for low-income apartments in Aurora, a suburb of Denver. They were new and available. I memorized the number with diligence and intended on calling this afternoon. If I could find a temporary place to live, the rest would fall into place. I also had to find a way to leave him without instigating a fight that would inevitably get out of hand. Self-control was not something he had a lot of these days.

I stepped out into the back yard and sat on the cool cement steps. The grass was a collage of browns and greens, the garden overgrown, and weeds grew around the swing set Nicholas had put up for Abby in the spring. We all have an idea of what we want our lives to be and the only person I know that it's worked out for is Megan. I closed my burning eyes and pictured a world of my own design. I would live in a little house with a big yard and a beautiful little garden. My husband would be compassionate, dependable, and most importantly he would want the best for me, allow me to be myself and love me for who I am. I would be a caterer with my own little shop right in town and Abby wouldn't be afraid to be a little girl. I opened my eyes again and sighed. That life was a long way off.

I thought of Jack, our meeting on the plane and in the bar. I had never met a man like him. I could tell he would be the type of man that would love selflessly. I knew I would never see him again and it wasn't that I *wanted* him. I wanted what he represented, the possibility of selflessness in a relationship. Years ago, I thought that's who Nicholas was or maybe it was me who wanted it so badly, that I created my own illusions. Either way it left me here, lonely and scared regretting selfish decisions and wanting something more.

Nicholas might think he has me where he wants me, but he doesn't. That is *his* illusion. I know who I am now and I just need to keep telling myself that I am a confident woman and a good mother. I cannot allow him to dictate when we can eat or how much money I have or especially how I feel about myself.

I stood up taking in the warm August air feeling dizzy and nauseous. *Let it begin.*

By the time Abby was up from her nap I had spoken with the apartments and had a plan.

"Ready to go for a little ride?" Abby clapped, she loved riding in the car.

I drove to a new bank setting up an account with only my name on it, requesting that they not send anything to my home address. My deposit consisted of the money I had earned at the Fuller wedding. It wasn't much but it was a start. Megan would also be wiring money to the new account to help me get started. I stopped at the grocery store picking up cheese, bread and milk. I also faxed the apartment application requesting a three or six-month lease giving them Megan's phone number. Abby and I spent some time at the park feeding the ducks and playing games on the grass. I hated lying to Nicholas but it was only for our protection. I simply didn't trust him anymore.

73 - Nicholas

Rebecca seemed to have found a new purpose without catering in her life and she almost looked at ease again. It was good to see her beautiful smile and I had told her so. As I came down the stairs, I saw that she already had breakfast on the table. She was usually asleep when I went to work so it was a nice surprise. She inquired about work and what was going on recently, did I still enjoy it, and how was Jerry treating me these days. It was flattering that she cared about what was going on in *my* life for once and we had a great conversation.

"I have to tell you Bec, its good to see you in the morning like this." She smiled at me and placed a plate of scrambled eggs and toast in front of me.

"Well, thanks. I have a busy day today so I thought I would get started."

"Oh yeah? What do you have going on?" The conversation was a relief but foreign in nature as we are usually fighting about something.

"Well, I have to go grocery shopping for one, I'm sure you noticed the fridge is looking a little sad."

"Yes, I was going to mention that."

"Then I have to…" She went on with her endless list of chores and errands. I lost track after the first three.

"Sounds like you have a full day." I cleaned my plate and stood up collecting my keys and bag.

"Gotta go Bec, this was delicious. See you tonight."

"Oh, Nicholas. I'm gonna need some money for groceries and some other stuff unless you'd rather come with after you get off work."

That was the *last* thing I wanted to do. I would give her access to the account in time but for right now it was necessary, though I must admit, inconvenient. I gave her three hundred dollars. "Spend it wisely." I joked.

I looked up at the house through the dirty windshield of my truck and shook my head in disbelief. Becca was coming around. I was thankful that we could finally get things back to normal. I knew she would understand that she was needed at home once her mind wasn't clouded with the catering business.

74 - Rebecca

Nicholas handed me three hundred dollars. I smiled innocently but inside I felt cynical *oh thank you so much for my allowance.* Abby and I went to Wal-Mart and I bought enough clothes to last her the next six months as well as a pair of shoes that wouldn't fit her quite yet but I wanted to have on hand for later. I was as thrifty as I could be trying to pick from the clearance racks. I would tell Nicholas that I spent one hundred dollars on Abby but I only spent $54.28 and would deposit the rest into my new *freedom account,* as I liked to think of it. The groceries I couldn't lie about but I would shop with the future in mind getting things I could bring with me that would get me started.

Grocery shopping was the last thing we did before going home and Abby was getting tired and cranky. I was feeling worn out as well and neither of us had eaten lunch yet so our stomachs were demanding to be fed. Thank God for hot dogs and macaroni and cheese. I started cooking as soon as I got home and would cut up some fruit for both of us to go with it. We both loved fruit but couldn't always afford to get as much as I would like. Nicholas didn't like anything healthy so it was really just for Abby and I and if he would have been shopping with us, he would have said something like *we don't need that, I'll never eat it. It's a waste of food.* As if he was the only one in the house!

I peaked around the corner at Abby watching a My Little Pony movie and continued to unpack the groceries. Just then the phone rang. I hoped it wasn't Nicholas. I really didn't have the energy for him right now. I took a deep breath and answered.

"Hello?"

"Rebecca Mitchell?"

"Yes, this is Rebecca Mitchell. Who is this?"

"Rebecca, my name is Howard Felt, I'm the chaplain at Montana Women's Prison and I have here on the phone with me Gary Poland, the warden."

My knees went weak and I felt dizzy and nauseous again. I pulled a chair over to me and took a seat preparing myself for the worst. "What happened?"

"Rebecca, your mother, Eveline Kerner committed suicide on Monday, August 12th. One of the guards discovered her after lights out. I'm so sorry."

I couldn't breathe. Why had she done this? She was so happy about the news from James. The last letter I got from her she was filled with joy and hope about the future. I don't understand. My sadness turned to anger at her selfishness. I still needed her! She can't be gone. *She can't be gone.*

"Rebecca? Rebecca are you still there?"

I tried to find my voice. "Ye- Yes. I'm here."

"I know this is a bad time ma'am but there are a few things to go over with you."

"How did she die?" The question came out on its own before I knew I was asking it.

"She hung herself." I broke into tears envisioning her dangling by a sheet or shoelaces in the middle of her cold, lonely cell in the dark. It filled me with utter sorrow and pity like none I had felt before.

The chaplain prayed with me even though I had no experience or knowledge of what I should say. I hadn't prayed properly since I was a child. He was able to help me collect myself and resume the conversation. The warden spoke of arrangements that needed to be made. Prisoners were not given funerals like people on the outside. He stated their routine for burying inmates in a cemetery outside the prison if there was no money for anything and that I could be present. I adamantly refused that she be put to rest in that fashion and gave him contact information for James and her Power of Attorney to get funding for a proper funeral. I explained that James and I would discuss the details and get back to him. I called James immediately after hanging up with the prison. The macaroni and cheese was done and I called Abby to the table while I stayed on the phone, trying to busy myself with the details and avoid falling apart.

"James, it's Rebecca."

"Oh, Becca, you heard. I'm so sorry." We both cried and consoled each other. I expressed confusion as to how this could happen. She was hopeful and happy.

"I feel responsible Becca."

"Why should you? Don't say that."

"I visited her about a week or so ago and she seemed happy to me too but we ended on a bad note. I'm afraid I upset her."

"James, it's not your fault." It hurt to think about what happened. I may never know why. "It was her decision."

Silence followed then James got down to business. He had a copy of her will in front of him. I had him wait on the phone while I dug through files for a copy of her will. She had given it to me *years* ago when she flew to Europe on a vacation saying that if she died in a plane crash or over seas it was important for me to have it. She wanted to be cremated and spread on the Rocky Mountains of Montana because she had always felt at home there. James reassured me that between him and her Power of Attorney they would take care of everything. He would email me a plane ticket as soon as he had all the details.

"Becca?"

"Yeah?" I responded breathless and tired.

"Your mother. Evy was a good person and I know she loved you more than anything."

"Thanks James."

"I'll call you soon."

I ran straight to the bathroom and vomited until there was nothing left. Abby padded into the bathroom in her little bare feet. "You okay Mommy?"

I wiped my mouth and drank water from the sink faucet. "Mommy's okay sweetie. Go finish your lunch."

~

Mom and I had climbed for what seemed like hours until we reached the top of a pine-tree covered mountain. I must have been nine or ten years old at the time. We walked up to the viewpoint and looked out upon the glorious space below us. *Pretend you're a bird and you're flying over these mountains, the cool wind against your face.* We put our arms out and closed our eyes. The white mountain peaks sparkled under the sun in the distance and green hills rolled along the valley leaving space for rivers and meadows. It looked like a magic fairyland to me. Mom said it was the only place she felt truly inspired.

~

I felt heavy as if rocks were tied to my wrists and ankles. It took every ounce of energy I had to get Abby down for her nap. I sat at the bottom of the stairs and cried with my head in my hands until everything went blurry. All of the sudden the air became thick and stifling and my lungs felt on the verge of collapsing. I stood up and bolted out the front door walking down the driveway not sure where I was headed. I stopped at the end and looked around me. People were driving in their cars, running errands, walking their kids down the street. A couple walked into the bakery on the corner. Somehow the world had continued on without me. I felt lonelier than I ever thought possible. It amazed me how, just when I thought it couldn't get any worse or feel any more disconnected, life proved me wrong – again. I decided to give myself a purpose to my presence at the end of the driveway by picking up the mail.

I sorted through it and froze when I saw Mom's handwriting on a white envelope. The back was stamped with the traditional prison information and I tore it open, thirsty for answers. The first paragraph was like a knife in the gut. The last time I had written her everything had been wonderful between Nicholas and I and the catering was going great. If she only knew now that I was falling apart and her absence now amplified the pain. I stopped short before continuing and felt thankful that she hadn't known my struggles. She had died knowing that I was okay and despite my emptiness, this gave me peace.

The remainder of the letter soaked through me like a dry sponge takes up water. She conveyed the frightening truth, trusting me with her soul. Her letter had a distinct sadness and a hidden farewell. I sank down against the inside of the front door and wept, her words haunting my thoughts. *Thank you for making me feel like I matter to you. I'll always love you.*

75 - Nicholas

The stale silence could be felt in the air as soon as I walked in the door. Abby was on the floor playing with blocks in front of the TV. Rebecca never let her watch TV in the evening. Something wasn't right. I came around the corner and dropped my stuff on the floor. Becca was crumpled up on the kitchen floor against the kitchen counter like a piece of worn-out notepaper. In her tear-soaked hand she held a letter she must have read a hundred times by the look of it.

"Becca?" I rushed over kneeling in front of her. She looked up at me as if I had just appeared out of nowhere searching my eyes for something but not finding what she was looking for.

"Mom's dead."

I took her in my arms like a child and rocked her. She spoke in fragments of suicide, a letter and of a funeral in the mountains of Montana. I held onto her and stroked her silky dark hair, "Everything will be okay. I'm here now. It's okay."

76 - Megan

As if she didn't have enough problems already, Eveline had to go and complicate things. Not that I should blame her for goodness sake, she had had enough problems of her own too. All Becca and Abby needed was some stability in their lives, was that too much to ask?

I was defensive for Rebecca's sake. How could Eveline been so lost that she could only think of herself? I had no idea what it felt like to be Becca right now, but I knew she had to be hanging on by a thread, hoping that by the time it all unraveled there would be someone there to catch her. On the phone her voice was quiet and short with little emotion. She clung to my words but was despondent and disappearing into another world with each passing moment.

I tried to keep her focused on the task-oriented details because nothing else seemed possible. She would fly out to Missoula with Abby and I would meet them at the airport. We would meet James at the church then follow him and a few other family members to Blue Mountain Lookout. There would only be a few people attending, making it a simple memorial.

Becca said she might want to say something at the memorial but wasn't sure and I told her she should do what ever she felt at the moment. She didn't want people to remember Eveline as a convicted murderer but as a loving mother and dedicated woman who made a difference in a lot of young people's lives through her teaching. Becca would know what she wanted to say when the time came.

Eveline was just a child in a woman's body, insecure and forsaken, trying to fit into her own skin.

77 - Rebecca

It was done. There was no going back now, or at least that's what I keep telling myself. It just so happened that Nicholas would be served the divorce papers while I was attending Mom's funeral. I didn't plan it that way. To be honest I would rather be in town so that we could talk about things and maybe settle things somewhat peacefully. I know he will think that I planned it but let him think what he wants. I have no ill intentions, just to stay true to myself and to give Abby the life she deserves. Not to mention, I don't have the energy to care what he thinks.

I drove to the park to walk for a while before I returned to Tracy's to pick up Abby. I walked barefoot in the grass and let the burden of all that was going on settle around me. *Get comfortable, it's going to be a long ride.* I should have stopped myself but I couldn't help but think of all the good times we've had, of all that I would be losing. I would miss knowing that someone else was with me, even if it wasn't constant, helping me deal with life's curves. I thought of Nicholas holding me on the kitchen floor and how we fit together. For once he was there to catch me when I fell apart and I would no longer have that option. What if I'm wrong? What if I'm making another mistake and putting Abby through this again for nothing?

There were bad times too. Many more bad times than good and I guess that's how I know it's the right thing to do. It's just more difficult to do the right thing when it's the hardest thing. The wrong thing is so much easier. I had to call Megan for reassurance once more when Abby and I got home. Megan is so good at telling me what I should do without actually telling me. I only realized this recently but she will ask me questions like, what do I want? Why? What do I think I deserve? Same for Abby? She has a way of making me realize what I already know. She also had a brilliant idea that gave me a new sense of hope. I would never have been brave enough to think of it on my own, never mind act on it. She thought that once our divorce was final and we had arranged how time with Abby would work out, she and Jeff would help us find a new home in Arizona close to her. I cried upon the very suggestion and she made me laugh. *See you tomorrow.*

Another funeral. My mother's funeral. I had hoped I wouldn't have to endure this experience again for at least twenty years or so but life isn't fair and it turns out death isn't either. Abby and I met Megan at the Missoula airport. We were elated and clung to each other crying in joy and sadness all at once.

She knelt down to see Abby. "You are such a big girl now! Oh my goodness."

"Auntie Megan!"

"That's right baby." She had never met Megan but ever since she was a baby, I would show her pictures of both Megan and Jeff and we often FaceTime.

"Finally, we get to meet in person and I can kiss those chubby cheeks!" We laughed and walked to baggage claim to collect our things. Abby would have time for a short nap at the hotel, if I was lucky, then we would have to meet James at the church. Abby was growing up so fast. She would be in school soon.

"How ya doin'?" asked Megan.

"I'm okay," nothing was a secret anymore. All the cards were out on the table and it felt good to live openly and to not have to justify anything anymore. I was much too tired. "It's a lot to take in. Nicholas should be getting the paperwork tomorrow some time so I'm holding my breath on that."

"Ugh, I guess it's probably good that you guys are here. It will give him time to cool down and think about things. You know how he gets when he isn't the one in control."

Do I *ever*! All the terrifying moments returned to me in a rush and confidence in my decision was reaffirmed.

I decided not to wear black to her funeral. As I explained to Megan it just didn't make sense to me and I didn't care what anyone else thought. Mom's favorite color was blue so that's what I wore. Abby was dressed in a pale blue summer dress with short sleeves and tiny deep blue flowers around the hem. I wore a navy-blue linen shirt with a pale blue tank top underneath and matching linen pants. Megan styled my hair in gentle curls pulled up to the side. The air was hot and smoke rose off the mountains in the distance. Montana was known for its consuming wildfires and this summer, from what I have heard, has been one of the worst, causing major highways to close for short periods of time.

We arrived at the church right on time. My stomach was in knots and I was sweating in places I didn't know I could sweat. My throat was swollen and tight. I dropped Abby off at the playroom, set up by the church for all the kids so they didn't have to sit through the memorial service, which I hoped would be short. I don't think I can bear this day to be any longer than it has to be. Memories of Mom had plagued my mind since the day I heard the shattering news and I couldn't help but picture her standing in the corner of the room watching everyone mourn. I mourned for her and for myself because I was the one left here all alone to sort things out for myself. Even though I still harbored so much anger toward her, I was doing my best to understand why she chose to leave me here without her.

James approached us, dark circles under his eyes and thinner than the last time we met. I hadn't even thought of what he must be feeling and his position saddened me but I didn't have the strength to take on his grief in addition to mine. I introduced Megan and after the pleasantries he became oddly silent.

"Rebecca, do you mind if I speak with you for a moment?"

I looked at Megan, scared for the next blow and needed her reassurance. She nodded, "I'll just go sit down toward the front there."

"It should be starting in a few minutes. We'll meet you up there." James assured her and walked me to the back corner of the church.

"Rebecca, I've been thinking a lot about your mother and about our conversation before – well I haven't been able to sleep much."

"James, it's not your fault. You don't need to explain anything."

"Yes, I do. I don't know if it has anything to do with what she did but I won't be able to live with myself if I don't tell you the whole story."

"Okay." What *was* it with people having to divulge all their secrets to me?

"Toward the end of our visit I gave Evy an update regarding the inheritance." Something had changed? She didn't mention this in her letter and frankly I was surprised since I knew it was important to her. "I let her know that although there would still be money it could only be used for her mental healthcare and nothing else. Dad was deemed incompetent due to his declined mental status. He was confused and didn't understand what he was doing when he stated she could inherit her share. I told her-," he broke off and looked away from me, obviously ashamed. "- that she was on her own for everything else, you know, living expenses and things of that nature."

I read between the lines and things became clear. James, being the executor, had contested and implemented these changes for, what I can only assume, his benefit. I could feel Mom's anger, depression and hopelessness at the reception of this news. She must have been devastated and lost. I looked back at James and remembered her mother's funeral and the deep despair of the entire family. She killed their mother and they wanted to help her but they didn't feel she deserved equal benefits from her death. I was conflicted in where my loyalties lied because I understood what both James and Mom needed and why. They were both right; and they were both wrong.

"I see."

"Anyway, I'm sorry Rebecca. I just thought you should know."

"Thanks James." There was nothing left to say between us. We reached a delicate, regrettable understanding.

I stood there in the corner as the music started and Megan looked back at me, beckoning me to join her. Words of my mother's letter echoed in my ears. *We are all colliding with each other in pursuit of our own agendas but I think we all really want the same thing – to matter to someone.* These are the words I repeated during the memorial as I paid tribute to her and to her life.

78 - Nicholas

A heavy knock on the door startled me. It's 6:30 in the morning! Who the hell could it be? I opened the door with force, angry at the disruption of my morning routine. I have never been much of a morning person. A small man in his fifties looks up at me with no emotion, "Are you Nicholas Alan Mitchell?"

"Yeah, who the hell wants to know? Did you know that it is six thirty A.M.!"

He hands me an envelope addressed to me and says, "Sir, you've been served." He asked me to sign for it then simply turns and walks away as if he had nothing to do with the disastrous disintegration of my life. I stood there with the door open looking at a white envelope not quite understanding what just happened. I slammed the door and ripped it open devouring the words. She wants a *divorce*!? Where the fuck did this come from? My body filled with rage and my heart ached. I threw the papers to the ground and grabbed everything I could find hurling it against the wall and the floor hoping to release this tension that took up every fiber of my being. I screamed and leaned against the damaged wall breathing hard.

We were *fine*. She was happy. She needed me. Just the other night in the kitchen I held her while she cried and it felt like we had connected again. How could she lie to me like this? I was there for her, I gave her my support, money, everything and this is how she repays me?! None of it made sense to me. We had some tough times in the past month or so but we've had tough times before and it always worked out.

It's eight o' clock in the evening and a fifth of Jack Daniels keeps me company as I wait for Becca to call. I decided to remain as composed as possible because over-reacting wasn't going to get her back. She'll realize she's making a mistake, even if it takes a few days.

"Nicholas?"

"Yep, that's me. What's up?"

"I was just calling to let you know that Abby is in bed and she's doing well. She said she misses you." I let silence fill the space between us hoping it made her uncomfortable. She had to know. "I'll be back in Denver tomorrow afternoon. Are you okay?"

"Oh me? Hey, I'm great! I just received a letter this morning. Any thoughts on what it might be?"

"Nicholas-."

I didn't let her finish, "Becca? What is this about? I thought things were going just fine." I took a deep breath.

"Nicholas, it wasn't my intention for you to receive it while I was gone, it just happened that way and I'm sorry."

"Well, that makes it all better." Why shouldn't I be cynical?

"C'mon Nicholas, things haven't been *fine*. They are not *fine*."

"What's the problem? I didn't pick up my clothes the other day? I forgot to take the garbage out? What is it this time Bec?"

"Oh yeah, that's the reason I'm asking for a divorce. Forgetting to take out the garbage is right underneath infidelity and controlling asshole on the list of reasons!" I was stunned by her confidence and cynicism.

"Infidelity? What the hell are you talking about?"

"Just because you won't admit it doesn't mean it didn't happen. I know you and Jenna have something going on or at least had something going on."

"Nothing happened Becca, stop being so paranoid."

"I don't believe you Nicholas. I saw the phone bill. I'm not as stupid as you think I am."

"We were just talking."

"I'm hanging up now."

"Can't we talk about this Bec? You don't want to do this."

"Don't tell me what I want Nicholas. Abby and I will be living in an apartment in Aurora temporarily until everything is settled."

"You can't have it all Bec, Abby is mine. Come to think of it so are you."

"No, Abby is *ours* and I was never yours. You'll be able to see her. I would never take her away from you. It's just better this way until everything is decided. I'll see you at the hearing." She hung up without saying goodbye.

I leaned back in my chair and smiled at her compassion. She'll come back. She always comes back.

79 - Rebecca

"I think this is the last trip Abby!" It's been a long week. My new apartment is finally starting to fill up and resemble a home. I recruited Tracy, Jen and Hannah to assist me in moving all of our things from the house to the apartment, while Nicholas was at work. I couldn't have done it without them. They were all supportive of my decision and said if I needed anything else to ask but they would be checking in on me from time to time. We were driving back to our new home with a car full of small odds and ends that were left at the house. Nicholas has tried to contact me several times, leaving both angry and pleading messages. I have let him talk to Abby a few times but I haven't had much to say to him. I didn't really expect him to be this angry and I was hoping he would just get over it with a little time to cool off.

Abby has been throwing more tantrums at the smallest of things and starting to show a little attitude. I know part of it comes with the job but I also know that she is missing a stable, consistent environment. *Hold on baby, we're getting there. I promise.* When I'm not working at the deli I spend as much time with her as I can but she is struggling adjusting to the day care. In the solace of the night, I can't help but feel like I'm failing. The hearing would be in a few days. I prayed and hoped that I could make it one more day and the next day I wished for the same thing.

I poured myself some tea and tiptoed to her room. She was looking older everyday and it amazed me that the little baby I once cradled is now a little girl full of words and questions. The sun would be coming up soon and the darkness in her room was changing to a faint blue glow. I still felt sick to my stomach every morning and was beginning to wonder if it wasn't something more than rattled nerves and stress. I opened the bathroom drawer and pulled out a pregnancy test I had purchased at the store yesterday evening on our way home. I dreaded the thought of it even being a possibility but I had to know. The seconds ticked by, the only sound echoing like a gong against the bathroom walls. I looked at the test and burst into tears. I held back the need to cry loud and hard, swallowing my disbelief. I threw it in the trash and stood up to examine my red tear-stained face in the harsh fluorescent lighting. *It's your responsibility Becca, deal with it.* I wasn't sure how I could handle having another baby, especially with Nicholas, but maybe he didn't have to know just yet. I wasn't ready to deal with this. I knew if I told him it would just give him more reasons to convince me that I needed him. *I don't need you Nicholas.* I looked deep into my own eyes. *I can do this without you. I can do this without you.*

80 - Nicholas

She wore black pin-stripe pants with a white button-down shirt and a matching suit jacket. She looked so beautiful and so professional. I had never seen her this way before and it made my desire for her grow. I came here with the intention of showing my best side. If I simply disagreed with this whole divorce thing and the judge saw me then how could he or she make us get a divorce? I would do or say whatever-I had to, to make this work. Both Becca and I had decided to represent ourselves, probably both assuming two things. One, neither of us had much money and two, I think we both thought it would be quick for different reasons. I sat down at the table across from her. Jen was in the audience holding Abby. I gave my daughter a little wink and she smiled back at me.

I was feeling hot and claustrophobic in my own professional attire. There were times I wore a tie to work but today was different. It was one of those moments that would change my life forever and the significance of it felt heavy on my chest. I looked down at the empty table and shook my head in disbelief that I was even here in court at a divorce hearing, again. I suppressed my anger at her audacity.

"All rise, the honorable Judge Wheyman presiding." We all stood up and sat down as he took his seat. I was thankful to see a man as our judge. I had a feeling that if it was a woman, I would be screwed from the moment she looked at the divorce paperwork, which I admit I did not read all the way through. It looked like a bunch of legal mumbo jumbo and I figured I would hear it again at the hearing anyway. We had been through this once before, nothing new.

Judge Wheyman stated the case and diligently reviewed every item of interest in the paperwork in front of him. He verified our agreement or disagreement on everything from dividing assets to caring for the "child of the marriage" to reasons for our separation. I promptly disagreed to her reasons for separation. Becca had stated infidelity, verbal abuse, physical abuse, and irreconcilable differences and I wasn't about to consent to any of that.

"Hell no, I don't agree!"

"Mr. Mitchell." The judge gave me a look of warning.

"Sorry your Honor. I disagree. I think that our differences *are* reconcilable." I looked over at Becca who looked shocked and horrified. I could tell she hadn't expected me to put up a fight. The judge proceeded to go down the list.

"Do both parties agree to the request on behalf of the petitioner, Rebecca Mitchell that she will be able to relocate to a permanent and stable residence outside of the state of Colorado providing the marriage is found to be irretrievable broken?"

"Yes, your Honor," said Becca all too eagerly.

My head snapped up, my eyes wide with astonishment. What is she trying to pull? "Are you kidding?" I turned to Becca who had her head down staring at her lap. "What are you doing? You can't leave! You can't take Abby out of the state! Why are you doing this to me?"

"Mr. Mitchell, one more outburst and I will hold you in contempt of court. That is your final warning."

I composed myself, my body buzzing with outrage. "Yes, your Honor. My apologies, but this is quite a shock and I definitely do *not* agree."

"Did you not read the documents served to you? None of this should be a surprise Mr. Mitchell. Frankly, Mr. Mitchell if any of the statements in these documents are found to be true and verifiable, my recommendation is that you rethink your position." I caught a faint smile spread across Becca's face in the corner of my eye. Okay, that's great. Humiliate me in front of everyone. I get it.

I mumbled under my breath. "Yes, your Honor."

Judge Wheyman sat in silence for three agonizing minutes while I stewed in my growing anger and trembling in anticipation. Finally, he spoke.

"Due to the denial by Mr. Nicholas Mitchell that the marriage is irretrievably broken, the court will request to continue this matter further at a second hearing. All relevant facts will be reviewed and at the future hearing the court shall make a finding as to whether the marriage is irretrievably broken. This hearing will be set for October 20th, 35 days from today at nine a.m. If no decision can be made at that time, the court will recommend that you both obtain counsel. Court is adjourned."

It was a temporary win for me and, feeling a small return of power, I glanced over at Becca with an air of confidence and pride. She steadied herself on the table then lowered herself back into the chair. She methodically collected her things and stood up with new resolve and feigned confidence. I met her halfway, stopping her from continuing down the aisle.

"I'm all you have Becca. I'm the only one who will be there for you." She looked up at me, her eyes glossy and rattled. "You can't do this without me and you know it. How are you going to support Abby? Just come back home, we can work things out."

"I never needed you Nicholas. I can do it without you." She took Abby's hand and walked away from me with Jen at her heels.

"You're gonna regret this Becca!" I thought that would stop her but she didn't even pause, she just kept walking until she disappeared from my sight.

81 - Rebecca

It was just days before the final hearing in which the court would determine if our marriage was 'irretrievably broken'. The term was somewhat morose but I suppose they had to pick something. How do you describe a marriage that has dissolved into a tangle of fear, control and illusions of a perfect life all turned to dust? There are no words that can describe what we have become and none to fix what has been done, except to find a way to start over. I was floored by the court's decision. I really thought it was all going to end that day and that I could try to move on with my life and help Abby move on with hers. All I could do now and all I have been doing for weeks is to cling to a thread of hope that Judge Wheyman will look at the documentation thoroughly and understand the predicament that I am in. After the hearing, I realized that Nicholas was going to fight this all the way. He didn't want me back, he just wanted to win.

I couldn't wait to feel the Arizona sun on my face and to be close to friends that love and know me, but I feared it would remain a dream, never coming to fruition. I've oscillated back and forth between feeling depressed and hopeless to positive and confident. I've had dreams where the judge decided that we would be forced to stay married and I could never live anywhere else but Denver. I would wake up sweaty and shaky having to double-check the calendar to make sure the dream wasn't real. I had requested this day off a couple of weeks ago when Megan surprised me saying her and Jeff would be flying out to support me at the final hearing. If it went well, she would help organize the relocation to Arizona and if it didn't then she and Jeff would help with getting a lawyer and whatever else I needed. I cried when she told me. Abby and I have been counting the days until their arrival. Jeff and Megan continued to be an example to me of what love could and should be like and it was encouraging to see the easiness between them. Now, the day was finally here that I would see them. It felt good to have a friend that would be there for me no matter what. Megan could be blunt but she was my only true friend I could depend on and trust unconditionally.

Abby wanted to build a fort after lunch, my all-time favorite game to play with her, especially now that she was getting older. We stacked pillows and I hung blankets over furniture. The rule was that we couldn't step on the floor because that was where the alligators were, but you could walk on the pillows to travel around the fort. Abby and I were cooking up some alligator stew when we heard a loud knock on the door. I looked at her surprised that Jeff and Megan were early. They had just called me from the airport and weren't due for another ten minutes.

"Is that Auntie Megan and Uncle Jeff?"

"Yeah!"

"Yeah!" I crawled out of the fort and opened the door swiftly without looking in the peephole. I was shoved backwards, the air from my lungs being forced out by the ground below.

"You're going to regret the day you left me."

82 - Jeff

Driving to Denver to help Becca pick up the pieces of a mess that she helped create wasn't exactly my idea of a vacation but it was important to Megan so it was important to me. Megan is the most selfless person I know and it's one of the qualities I love most about her. Sometimes though, other people's problems consume her and she begins to take them on as her own. This is usually when I step in because I want to protect her from inevitable self-destruction. Megan is my weakness. I would go anywhere with her and do anything for her. All she has to do is look at me with those beautiful green eyes and I melt. I love Becca like a sister. She's been a part of our lives for years and Becca and Abby have become more like family. I hate seeing her hurt but I think you also have to let people make their own decisions despite what you might think. Sometimes it takes falling on your face a few times before you figure out who you are.

I'm really not sure what Becca ever saw in Nicholas. He was a thin-framed man with more weight on his body than it was meant to handle. He's slightly taller than Becca but if she wore heels and stood confidently, she rose above him, which he didn't like much. Looks certainly aren't everything but the man's personality is atrocious and you would think that would have been the kicker, the red flag saying *no, stay away*. Maybe she misread the signs, I'm not sure but she kept going back for more, year after year. When they were divorced the first time I thought *Yes! Finally!* An end to the drama and maybe her and Abby had a shot at a decent life.

Then naturally, Becca had to go back for more, punishing herself for reasons I would never understand no matter how much Megan tried to explain it to me. Something about self-esteem and control in an abusive relationship. I don't know much about that stuff but I do know that common sense should kick in somewhere. If the common sense didn't kick in then the motherly instinct should and maybe that's why Becca had chosen to leave him a second time. I was crossing my fingers that this separation would last more than six months but I wasn't holding my breath. Evidently, Nicholas could be a persuasive man and Becca didn't have a lot of strength so it could be a deadly combination. I was hoping the court would rule in Becca's favor allowing us to continue on with the moving plan and go home a little sooner.

Megan and I drove into the parking lot of her new apartment in Aurora. It was a new complex with contemporary design and colors and a sparkling fountain in the entrance, something I didn't expect since it was a low-income building, but I was quite impressed at Becca's choice. We pulled into the parking spot as Becca had directed.

"Oh no." Megan said in almost a whisper. She stared out the window at the vehicle next to us on the passenger side.

"What?"

"I think that's Nick's truck. Shit!" She flew out of the car and I followed, running behind her.

We had a hard time finding the right door but I looked up and pointed it out to Megan. "There it is, apartment 203." Megan bolted up the stairs and my heart was racing with what ifs.

We arrived at the top of the staircase to find the door ajar. Megan hesitated slightly before pushing it open. We heard muffled screaming and crying. What struck me the most, was the *way* she screamed. It wasn't just a fight, there was a desperation and pleading to her voice that sent chills throughout my body. I caught up to Megan just as she pushed open the door and stepped in.

Becca was in the corner of the living room balled up crying and begging for Nicholas to stop. Her hair was wild and her clothes torn and bloody. Nicholas was kneeling over her punching her anywhere he could find her vulnerable. My senses seemed to heighten and my body buzzed with adrenaline. I noticed Abby across the room, she was crying and looked terrified of the scene in front of her. All of the sudden she darted toward her parents stepping only on the pillows. My heart sank knowing that she had to witness this horrific moment. Megan ran toward Becca just as Abby started hitting her dad.

"Daddy, stop it." She was crying and not sure what else to do. I tried to call out to her telling her to come to me but she didn't hear me. "Don't hurt Mommy! Stop it!" Nicholas reacted shaking Abby off and shoving her fragile body to the ground. Abby fell hard, her head hitting the end table and her body lay lifeless in between two pillows.

Megan took advantage of his hesitation as he looked over at Abby and immediately placed herself between Becca and Nicholas. I heard Nicholas apologize to Abby under his breath then step back in surprise at our presence. He backed up looking at Megan, then at me. I walked toward him trying to hide my fear.

He screamed at Megan. "Always here to *save* her. Well, she doesn't need saving! She needs me!"

I interrupted with as calm a voice as I could muster. "Nick. Let's think about this okay. Don't do this." Megan was on her knees now in front of Becca with her arms up in the air as if to form a shield in front of Becca. There was no trace of fear in her eyes, only a protective anger.

He pulled a gun from the back of his pants and cocked it pointing it directly at Becca. "She's going to take everything away from me!"

Megan and Becca screamed and shuddered at the sight of the gun. My first thought was Megan, if anything happened to her at his hand, I swear I would kill him myself. "Nick! You don't know that man. The hearing is tomorrow, I'm sure you guys can work something out." I took slow deliberate steps toward him. "It doesn't have to be like this. If you do this, you *will* have nothing. You still have a chance."

Becca screamed for Abby, "What did you do to my baby!"

"*You* did this!" He screamed. "This is all *your* fault. Look at what you've made me do! Why couldn't we just be happy together?" His voice changed from anger to an eerie, sinister tone that made me cringe. Right then and there I knew what he was capable of. He would go as far as he needed to get what he wanted.

There was silence, everyone breathless not knowing what to do next. I thought maybe if Megan could distract him, I could try to wrestle the gun from him. It was a long shot but that was all we had. I made eye contact with Megan, speaking to her without words. I told her I loved her and shifted my eyes toward Nicholas to signal a distraction. She gave a slight nod.

"Nicholas, maybe you could still be happy together." I was disgusted at the sound of her words but Megan was smart and he seemed to be buying it for now. "Maybe you can still be together." Becca looked shocked and repulsed not realizing at first what Megan was trying to do. She kept looking over nervously at Abby sprawled on the floor. "Not like this. Okay?"

Just when he seemed to be thinking about Megan's proposal, I lunged in his direction taking him to the ground with me. The gun went off but I couldn't see where the bullet had gone. Nicholas shot again, blindly in defense after landing a punch on my left eye. I fought back punching him hard in the face and stomach. The gun fell out of his hand and he pushed me back with his second wind. I fell on my back and out of the corner of my eye I saw Megan and Becca lying on the floor. If she's hurt, I'll kill him. I knew I had to keep him down. I brought my legs up and twisted them with his, snapping his knee. As he arched back screaming in pain, I threw him to the ground, grabbed his throat with one hand and punched him as hard as I could with the other. Blood seeped down his face and his body went limp. I stopped, surprised at my own strength and let him fall to the floor breathing hard. I lifted my head at the faint sound of sirens and remembered Megan and Becca.

I ran to her side. "Megan! Baby, are you okay?" Becca knelt over her body with Abby cradled in her arms.

She looked at me, tears and blood streaking her face. "Jeff." Her eyes moved down Megan's body. Blood covered her shirt. She had been shot, her abdomen oozing. I told Becca to put pressure on the wound and I took Megan's head in my hands. *No, I can't do this without you.* "Stay with me Megan! It's gonna be okay. I'm here." It wasn't okay, my heart was crumbling and my insides felt like they were on fire. The ground was dissolving underneath my body and I couldn't find my footing. All of the sudden, she opened her eyes and looked at me squeezing my hand and my world came back into focus.

"Is he gone?"

Tears poured down my face at the sight of her beautiful eyes, "Yes baby, he's gone. Everything's gonna be okay now. You did so great."

"I love you."

"I love you too. Always." Her grip loosened and her eyes went calm.

Becca was crying in the background, "No, Megan. No."

Everything was falling down around me. I couldn't grasp what had just happened. In this fleeting moment so much had gone wrong and I wasn't able to stop it. I wasn't able to save her. I was overcome by anger at Nicholas and his petty selfish rage. I looked behind me to see him bent over Abby crying. He looked up and held my eyes realizing what he had done and the how the room filled with anguish so heavy it was difficult to breathe.

Becca looked down at her beautiful little girl then over at Meagan. A strength seemed to fill her like I have never seen before. She stood up and began screaming at Nicholas. "Look what you did! You want me? Go ahead! Kill me! Is that what you want?!"

I held his stare but thrust my body forward in one attempt to gain control of the gun lying on the floor between us. He stood quickly and backed up against the back of the couch, hobbling on his good leg. Becca stood behind me stoically silent.

Her voice did not waiver. "Shoot him Jeff." Nicholas's eyes widened in Becca's direction. She spoke boldly, her words dripping with agony. "You did it, Nicholas. Congratulations, you took away everything that has ever mattered to me in my life."

My hand was shaking and I reached up with the other hand to steady it. The sirens were loud now and I heard footsteps on the stairs. I wanted so badly to end his life because he had just ended mine. I kept telling myself he deserved it for what he did. I glanced at Megan's lifeless body then back at the man who took away the woman who held the other half of my soul. I would never be whole again. I cocked the gun and fired, hitting the couch just to his left.

The door flew open, and police flooded the apartment. Becca screamed and I held the gun at Nicholas who appeared to be drowning in his own realization that he had lost.

The voices started to become more than just noise. "Sir, put down the gun!" I came to my senses. They would handle it now and I would make sure Nicholas would never see the light of day. He would suffer and dwell on the misery he had caused every day for the rest of his god-forsaken life. He would recount over and over how he lost his most prized possession – control. I slowly lowered the gun and dropped it. It bounced toward Nicholas and he looked at it briefly.

One policeman took a tentative step forward toward the gun. In one swift move Nicholas reached down and regained control pointing it at everyone. "Get back! I'll shoot!"

Everyone backed up but Becca who seemed to be stuck and unable to find the strength to move. He pointed the gun at Becca, her entire body shaking. Nicholas looked down at Abby then back at his wife. His voice did not waiver as he brought the gun to his head and pulled the trigger, a coward till the very end. "You'll always be mine."

83 - Rebecca

The palm leaves swayed and rustled in the warm breeze. Their fingers outstretched to one another shimmering in the sunlight. I loved the way they towered over me, protecting me. I stood next to Jeff at Megan's funeral. We had both lost the person who seemed to complete us and the hole left by her absence was unbearable and irreplaceable. Nicholas had taken away my best friend and my unborn child, but he had not won. The days had gone by in a blur and here I stood in front of Megan's coffin unable to speak or to comprehend why someone like her was allowed to be taken from this life. It was in that moment that my emptiness and heartache took on a new purpose. I would do my utmost to find a way to make her proud of me. She was my inspiration, everything I wished I could be. I vowed to be what she always knew I could be, the best version of myself.

Dressed in red, Megan's favorite color, I placed a red rose on her coffin steadying myself. The tears poured down and I had given up trying to hold them back. I turned to see Jeff. I had never seen a man filled with such sorrow and anguish. I knew he would ponder every move he made that day, wondering if he had done just one thing differently, would she still be alive?

I walked over to him, wiping tears from his cheek. "Jeff."

His eyes remained fixed on Megan, "I know. I'll see you around." We embraced each other holding on for dear life. I nodded and smiled in understanding.

I took Abby's precious little hand in mine and walked away without looking back.

84 - Jack

Every time I step out my door into the sunshine and warm desert air, I'm glad I made the decision to take this position as a copywriter/journalist for the Arizona Republic. I applied to a few different newspapers in the southwest region and the Republic offered me the best package; benefits, pay and more importantly a great living environment. It was time to move on with my life in a new place and it doesn't get any better than this. Today I am attending a fundraiser for Desert Winds Elementary, a school that has been getting a lot of publicity for its programs that help low-income families work to stabilize learning and social environments for children. The whole program is a brilliant idea and it would be my first story in Arizona.

I pulled up to the school taking in the brand-new tan stucco building with brown and sage green accents. Everything in the Scottsdale area has the same soothing desert colors and instead of grass and trees as landscaping, there are various colors of rock, sand, cactus and desert plants. Some people might find it boring and colorless but I thought it was the most beautiful place I had ever seen. Everything around me made sense for the first time in my life and it felt damn good. There was one exception but I would have to find a way to forget about her at some point, which I wasn't sure I would ever be able to do. A flag flew out front and there was a large green banner over the school entrance advertising the fundraiser. It was still early and people began to fill the parking lot and make their way toward the school bringing cookies and cakes for the masses. Why is it that no one ever brings healthy food to these things?

I patted my pocket to make sure I had my handy notepad and entered the school in search for Janice Trent, the principal of Desert Winds. The large tile entryway was the main setting for the event and I spotted Janice in the corner instructing various teachers and administrative staff on their roles.

"Mrs. Trent?" I approached her with my hand extended in greeting.

"Yes?"

"Hello, my name is Jack Lauson. We spoke over the phone once. I'm with the Arizona Republic."

"Oh, yes of course. Thank you for coming Jack." She went on to explain how the fundraiser would work and answered a few questions about the school and its goals in regards to the students and parents. She was a pleasant woman with short graying hair, delicately styled and turquoise earrings that matched her long colorful necklace most likely made by her young students. The space was filling up and I began to mingle around the crowd speaking to various parents, relatives and even children about their experiences at the school. I enjoyed the children the most as they are so innocently honest.

I was intently finishing some notes and looked up to interview the next person I bumped into, but instead I came face to face with Rebecca Mitchell.

"I –" I dropped my notepad and pencil and stood there like a dumbfounded bumbling idiot. How could this be? Am I still in Arizona or am I just imagining her? I studied her face and eyes knowing that it *was* her. I had dreamed about this many times, hoping as I went about my life in Denver that I would run into her again, in a coffee shop, at Les Schwab, at a bar, anything. But I had given up hope and forced myself to move on with my life and of all places I find her here.

"Becca? Is it really you?"

"Jack? Oh my God! I can't believe it's really you!" She jumped forward and threw her arms around me as if I was her lifeline. It was the first time we embraced and it felt like home, like I was meant to hold her and she was meant to be in my arms. We fit like a lock and key. It took me a moment to reciprocate, out of pure shock, but I wrapped my arms around her in return.

"It's so good to see you. I thought I'd never see you again."

"What are you doing in Arizona?" She asked.

"I could ask you the same question!"

We stood there a moment smiling at each other and I noticed a beautiful little girl standing next to her and knelt down in front of her. "Hey kiddo! What's your name?"

She looked up at her mother to get approval to speak to a stranger then smiled back at me, "Abby." She put her arms behind her back and swayed back and forth.

"Abby, my name is Jack," I put out my hand, "it's very nice to meet you!" She looked just like her mother. I looked up at Becca, her body a silhouette against the light.

"I moved here recently." I said, getting to my feet. I couldn't help but trip over my words. Something about her was different, more solid, more confident, and it drew me to her even more. "I took a job with the Arizona Republic in Arizona, here, and . . . and I'm doing a story on the school and it's programs for low-income families."

"Wow! Jack that's great."

"What about you?" She looked down at Abby and sadness crept across her face like I had never seen before. "I'm sorry. You don't have to answer. It's the reporter in me."

"No, it's just – I moved here just about a couple months ago. We love it don't we Abby!"

"I got to swim in a swimming pool!"

"Wow!" I said.

"Abby started kindergarten here if you can believe it. She's so grown up."

There was silence and the next question swelled between us like a burst of monsoon air. I couldn't ask but I was hoping she would say something.

"Abby? Why don't you go play with Isabel in the play room okay?" She ran off toward her friends skipping with excitement.

"Are you still catering?"

"You remembered!" She looked surprised and flattered, "I am working on starting a business here but it's slow. We're still getting settled and I'm trying to spend as much time with Abby as I can while trying to balance work."

"People will be begging for your services soon enough! I just know it." She blushed and smiled but a trace of misery crept across her face.

"Nicholas is gone." She blurted it out like air from a deflating a balloon.

I didn't know what to say. I was selfishly elated but unsure of the circumstances I held my breath. The strange thing was that her words had more anger in them than sadness. "I'm sorry Becca."

Becca met my eyes again. "Don't be sorry Jack."

She leaned into me and I held her as people poured around us, her tears wet on my shoulder. I smoothed her long dark hair and gently released her, wiping the wetness from her face.

"You okay?" It was then that I realized something horrible and tragic had happened. I saw not only sadness, but also a deep sense of regret for things that I was only beginning to understand.

"I'm more than okay." She paused and held my eyes. "I should have known it was you from the first time we met."

I was both stunned and relieved. I held my breath for a moment, letting the truth we had both ignored in the past settle between us.

"What would you and Abby say to getting some ice cream after the fundraiser? I know I would regret it if I let you disappear again." She stood there in a brief heart pounding silence, her eyes starting to brim with tears of a different kind and a smile broke across her face like a sunrise on the desert horizon.

"We love ice cream."

The End

Made in the USA
Coppell, TX
09 December 2021

67715562R00134